The Great Traits of Champions

Fundamentals for Achievers, Leaders, and Legacy Leavers

2nd Edition

The Great Traits of Champions

Fundamentals for Achievers, Leaders, and Legacy Leavers

2nd Edition

by

Mark Tewksbury

and

Debbie Muir

|GREAT|TRAITS|INC.

Library and Archives Canada Cataloguing in Publication

Tewksbury, Mark, 1968-
    The great traits of champions : fundamentals for achievers, leaders, and legacy leavers / by Mark Tewksbury and Debbie Muir. -- 2nd ed.

ISBN 978-0-9809083-1-2

    1. Achievement motivation. 2. Success--Psychological aspects. 3. Leadership. 4. Self-actualization (Psychology). 5. Motivation (Psychology). I. Muir, Debbie, 1953- II. Title.

BF503.T47 2011   158.1
C2011-906334-4

Developed and Produced by Focus Strategic Communications Inc.

Project Management: Adrianna Edwards
Developmental Edit: Ron Edwards
Interior Design: Val Sanna
Interior Layout: Nancy Szostak
Copyedit and Proofread: Linda Szostak

Cover Design by Emmanuel Bégin

Printed in Canada

www.thegreattraits.com

| GREAT | TRAITS | INC.

Table of Contents

Welcome to *The Great Traits of Champions*!

MARK: *As we get started, let me introduce you to my co-author, **Debbie Muir**. Debbie is one of the Olympic movement's most winning coaches. She led her athletes to win seven out of a possible nine World Championship gold medals, as well as two Olympic gold and two Olympic silver medals in the sport of synchronized swimming.*

DEBBIE: My co-author, **Mark Tewksbury**, is an Olympic champion, a three-time Olympic medalist, and seven-time world record holder in the sport of swimming. We both come from a high-performance sport background. Combined, we have many (many!) decades of experience in a movement that is rich with achievement, leadership, and legacy.

MARK: *In this book, we are going to share with you what we know; we will take you on the **Champion's Journey**. But first, you need to know some things about us. For starters, we do not think we know it all.*

DEBBIE: We *are not* gurus.

MARK: *We will not solve all of your life's problems by taking seven steps.*

DEBBIE: All we have is our collective experience. We *are* a coach and an athlete. We *have* lived what we speak. We *will* share with you how you can apply what we have learned from our experience into something meaningful for you.

The objective of this book is to lay out what we believe are the building blocks to succeed in the areas we have experienced extensively. What you decide to do with that knowledge is up to you.

MARK: *Coming from sport, the idea of being a champion is naturally a part of the culture. Champions are winners, the best; they reach the pinnacle. In this book, we take a broader approach. These traits can be applied to any number of areas in life, not just sport.*

DEBBIE: We look at the idea of being a champion from three distinct perspectives.

MARK: *First, we have the Achiever Traits. This section starts from the premise that every one of us wants to be the best we can be at whatever* *it is we are doing. This first part of the* Champion's Journey *ensures the fundamental ideas are in place to build the skills necessary for you to succeed. What do you want to achieve? What would be considered a win for you?*

DEBBIE: Then, we have the Leader Traits. Being a great achiever is one thing; being a great leader is another. In this section, you lay the foundation for others—individuals, teams, and organizations—to succeed. What does it take to create champion teams and organizations? What would you define as a winning result? How can you ensure that you bring out the best in those you lead? This is the second step in your *Champion's Journey*.

MARK: *And finally, we have the Legacy Traits. Achieving and leading are important, but it is equally vital to consider what kind of impact you are making along the way. Are your actions creating a win/win situation? What effect are you having in your world? What kind of ripple effect are you making? Legacy explores the fundamentals needed to make a meaningful and positive contribution, and shows you how to bring all of the traits together for ongoing success.*

Use This Book as a Guide to Being a Champion in Your Life

DEBBIE: We bet you live a busy life (because we all seem to these days!). We wanted to make sure this book was presented in a way that is easy to access. We don't want the Great Traits to be a burden, we want them to enhance your life.

MARK: *People often say there is a great connection between sport and life, and mean it in a more general, metaphorical sense. We explored that idea. What is it that, when stripped down to its absolute core, ensures excellence in achievement and leadership? What are the absolute fundamental principles that are relevant and transferable to any experience, endeavor, or organization? From that lens, an intense exploration of our experience was taken and, over time, the Great Traits were born.*

DEBBIE: There are eight traits in each section, for a total of 24. But don't let that intimidate you. There is nothing new in this book per se.

Instead, the following pages are filled with ideas you might know or recognize, organized in a logical, practical way that we believe will make them even more accessible to you.

MARK: *Each trait in this book includes an icon, key concept, anecdotes, and learning objectives that outline the fundamental ideas we want you to bring to life. Following each section, a simple evaluation tool will help you identify which of the traits you are already utilizing, and which ones need more attention. If you are looking for some guidance on where to tackle the traits, start there.*

DEBBIE: Mark and I have spent the past few years leading thousands of people through Great Traits programs. Although the book presents the traits in a linear fashion in order to discover them one at a time, the truth is that all of the traits work together. Mark and I often jump around and choose traits from the Achiever, Leader, and Legacy sections when designing programs based on an individual's or a company's needs. You will see as you use this book that the same will hold true for you. Because they are so essential and the learning is so clear, knowing the various Great Traits will help you quickly identify what learning is relevant to your situation.

MARK: *I used to think that to be really great at something, you had to master complicated concepts or skills. When I was among the best in the world, I was constantly looking out for something huge that would make a difference. It was only when I went back to some fundamental ideas I knew but had taken for granted that I made my breakthrough.*

DEBBIE: Whatever it is you are doing—whether you are a parent, a businessperson, a teacher, a communications expert, a volunteer, an agent, a member of a board, a co-worker, or a community activist—this book provides a foundation for success to be built upon. Within these pages is a frame of reference to make sure that you have all of your bases covered as you move through your life as an achiever, leader, and legacy leaver. We hope you enjoy it.

LET YOUR CHAMPION'S JOURNEY BEGIN!

The Achiever Traits

*Fundamentals for
Being a Champion*

Each of the Achiever Traits has a graphic icon highlighted in green to help support the key ideas found within. In keeping with the fundamental theme of the book, the images are simple and straightforward.

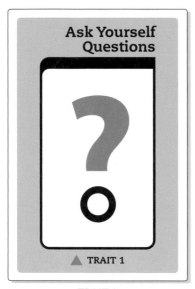

TRAIT 1:
The question mark reminds us
to ask ourselves questions.

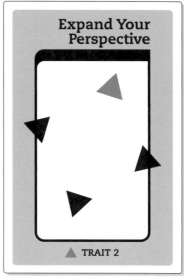

TRAIT 2:
The arrows outside of the box
represent an expanded perspective.

TRAIT 3:
The plan is leading toward a star—our
representation of your desired win.

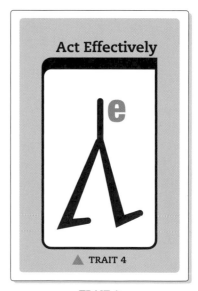

TRAIT 4:
A pair of walking legs with an 'e'
remind us to take 'e'ffective action.

Use all eight icons as visual reminders of the key concepts and ideas found within each of the upcoming Achiever Traits.

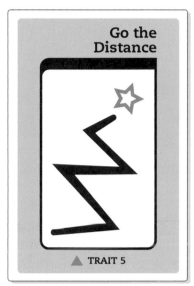

TRAIT 5:
The long, winding road leading to the green star represents enduring challenges.

TRAIT 6:
A blank slate represents innovation, making connections in new and creative ways.

TRAIT 7:
The thought bubble lifting a barbell reminds us to "work out" our mind.

TRAIT 8:
The beaming smile illustrates the infectiousness of attitude.

ACHIEVERS

Your *Great Traits Champion's Journey* begins here by mastering the Achiever Traits.

The first part of our book lays a rock-solid foundation from which any achievement can be reached. Being a champion from the Achiever perspective means that whatever it is you are doing, you can be your best, be top of your game, and accomplish great things.

In this section, we take you back to when the Great Traits were born. Over 20 years ago, in the final year of Mark's swimming career, he had to make a seven-year improvement in his event—in less than a year!—to achieve the goal of winning the Olympics. It was through this difficult experience that we met and began our own *Champion's Journey*. The magic of the Achiever Traits is that not only did we see them work in that Olympic year, but we continue to see that over time these ideas transfer directly to other situations, big and small, with equal relevance.

We have no right to tell you what to do, or how to live your life. We are simply two people from the world of sport who have found something to be universally true. Every single one of us has a chance to achieve whatever it is we want to. The objective of the Achiever Traits is to remind *you* of what is possible for yourself, and to share practical ways to make it a reality.

Whether it is being a top salesperson, being a great parent, giving an outstanding presentation, delivering a flawless musical performance, starting your own business, or reaching a personal goal such as stopping smoking, the fundamental ideas needed to reach all of these personal wins remains the same. This is what the Achiever Traits cover: What skills do you need to master to achieve your best?

Each Achiever Trait begins with us sharing a part of Mark's Olympic story with you. We then identify a key concept that describes what we mean for that particular trait. Following that, we have learning objectives and anecdotes that bring the trait to life. At the end, there is a Review section with a summary and exercises to help you practice that particular Achiever Trait.

Every one of us is asked to be great—our own version of a champion—in some way or another. By mastering the Achiever Traits, you not only build the foundation to achieve anything, you also build the foundation to master the next sets of traits.

Before you can lead and truly maximize the legacy you leave, you need to master the ideas necessary to achieve. Your *Champion's Journey* begins here and now.

Have fun!

TRAIT 1:

Ask Yourself Questions

KEY CONCEPT
By becoming a master of the question, you stay connected to yourself and to what you want to achieve.

DEBBIE: Our story begins at the Aquatic World Championships in Perth, Australia, a year and a half before the Barcelona Olympics. I was coaching the synchronized swimming team, and almost every day Mark would come over and watch us practice. Mark and I had known each other in passing for many years, but it was at this particular event that we started to become friends. Mark's 100-meter backstroke final was toward the end of the competition, so I had to rearrange my schedule to allow me to watch his race before flying home. I was so glad I did. He swam one of the most exciting races I had ever seen.

MARK: *I had been on the national team for seven years, but this was my breakthrough. At major international competitions in the past, I had always been fourth or fifth. This was certainly an achievement in its own right, but my dream of getting to the medal podium had always eluded me. I was always just a fraction of a second off. It was heartbreaking. At these World Championships, I finally broke that cycle.*

11

DEBBIE: No kidding! He almost won the race. It was thrilling to watch because Mark was behind the entire time, but he never gave up. He kept coming back on the leader, and at the end of the race, Mark was only six one-hundredths of a second behind Jeff Rouse, the world record holder, and he had won his first world championship medal, a silver. With 18 months to go before the Olympics, Mark was finally on his way.

MARK: *Or so it had seemed. Fast-forward seven months to the Pan Pacific Championships in Edmonton, Alberta. I was competing against Jeff again, but this time it was in Canada so I had the homefield advantage. It would be the last time that Jeff and I would race each other before the Olympic Games the following year in Barcelona. My family and friends all traveled to watch the competition. The energy around the pool that night was electric. But, instead of the come-from-behind victory I had envisioned, disaster struck.*

The noise was deafening as I finished the race. The crowd was going absolutely wild. The problem was that I knew in my gut when I hit the wall that they were not cheering for me. I looked up to the scoreboard and found my name. My time—55:29—was exactly the same as I had posted in Perth. In the months since the World Championships, my strategy had been simple—don't change a thing. Amazing how well that works—don't change a thing, get the same result.

Above my name was Jeff's and his time—53:93. He had chopped 1.2 seconds off his Perth result and smashed the world record. To put that in perspective, if you added up all of my incremental improvements over the seven years I had been on the national team, it came to 1.2 seconds. I now had less than 10 months to make the same improvement if I had any chance of winning the Olympics. That didn't seem possible. I went from a fingernail away from my dream coming true to having to do the impossible. I was shocked, then depressed, then scared out of my mind.

So what had happened? Following my breakthrough swim at the World Championships, I had thought that I was really on the right track with what I was doing. When I went back to my day-to-day routine, I got a bit complacent. I didn't question how I might do things better, or even why I was doing them. In my mind, I had arrived, and I had started to take things for granted. The only thing I might have asked myself was how great it was going to feel when I inched ahead of Jeff by six one-hundredths of a second the next time we raced. Unfortunately, this hadn't been the right question.

In silence, I drove home from the competition, my head swirling with questions. I asked myself over and over, "What just happened? How did it happen? What am I doing?" I needed to regroup, to get clear, to give myself some time to honestly assess how things had turned out this way, and what I was going to do next.

TO BE A CHAMPION:
1. Understand the Power of the Question
2. Know What to Ask Yourself When
3. Be Honest With Your Answers

ACHIEVERS

1. Understand the Power of the Question

Questioning is the fundamental skill set required for information gathering, problem solving, and decision making. It is an extremely important trait to master. Asking questions helps you face the facts about where you find yourself. Questioning connects you to reality, which can sometimes be brutal. It helps you find clarity and allows you to consider the implications of what will happen if you continue to do the same things, or what might happen if you do things differently. Such is the power of the question.

Many of us don't stop and think about what kinds of questions we are asking ourselves. We react to life as it unfolds, often not taking the time to reflect until something major happens. This first Achiever Trait puts you in the proactive mode. Becoming a master of the question means incorporating the simple skill of questioning into your life. Stop letting events just happen to you and start making them happen *for* you.

Keep in mind that different types of questions will lead you to different answers and different outcomes. We are concerned with two specific types of questions. The first type is soul searching, and is an internal process that helps you feel more connected to yourself and what you are doing. These are questions like the following:

▲ What am I doing?
▲ Why am I doing it?
▲ What is important to me?

The other type of question is more external, focusing on where you find yourself with respect to the world around you. These are questions like the following:

▲ Where do I stand in relation to the best?
▲ What do I have to do in order to improve my results?
▲ What do I need to do differently or what do I need to keep doing?

When you build on this trait, you will master both types of questions.

2. Know What to Ask Yourself When

It is so easy to take questions for granted. Start paying attention to the kind of questions you are asking to make sure you are asking POWERFUL questions that REVEAL useful information. As you make your way through this book, you will become more equipped to ask yourself better and better questions. Over time, you will know intuitively what to ask yourself, and when to ask it.

If your questions aren't serving you—if they are not getting you the information you need—consider asking yourself different questions. For example, instead of asking, "*Why* does this keep happening to me?" ask, "*What* can I learn from this so it doesn't happen again?" Choose a new starting point. The more you ask yourself questions, the better you get at asking yourself the *right question* at the *right time*.

3. Be Honest With Your Answers

Asking the right question is only the first step. Listening to the answers is next. You need to be brutally honest with yourself. Your answers will lead you to what you need to do, or if not, at least guide you to the next question to ask yourself. That sounds simple, but many of us try to screen ourselves from the truth. We don't want to face what is really going on because it might mean we have to change. But if we don't listen to ourselves honestly, we get stuck and start to spin our wheels. Through questions, you will discover what excites and interests you, what you will commit to, and what steps you need to take to make it happen.

The important thing to remember is that there are no wrong or right answers. Simply take the time to listen carefully for *your* truth. What is going on in your head? How do you feel? What do you really want? And where do you find yourself now? The answers might come quickly. In other cases, it might require some time for your truth to emerge. Enjoy taking that time in order to reflect and to listen to yourself. Ultimately, asking yourself questions leads to greater clarity and understanding.

DEBBIE: I have a friend who has a hard time settling into employment. She joins a new company, but within six months to a year the shine wears off and problems begin to appear. And these problems are similar to those that occurred in her last job. She goes into a company and at first everything is great. Then, she soon feels that people are turning against her. At first, I fully sympathized with her and supported her. But then the next job came along and the same thing happened all over again. When it occurred a third time a year later, I felt she really needed to ask herself some hard questions and answer them honestly. Instead of it always being about the employer and coworkers, she needed to ask the question, "What part am I playing in this?" Fortunately, she eventually did, and was able to face the harsh reality that her own behaviour was a large part of the problem. She was finally able to break this losing pattern and stay employed.

ACHIEVERS

ACHIEVERS

▲ TRAIT 1 REVIEW: Ask Yourself Questions

TO BE A CHAMPION:
1. Understand the Power of the Question
2. Know What to Ask Yourself When
3. Be Honest with Your Answers

KEY CONCEPT
By becoming a master of the question, you stay connected to yourself and to what you want to achieve.

REALITY CHECK!
We know that it can be kind of scary to ask yourself questions because you might not want to know the answers. Sometimes it is easier just to go on autopilot instead of facing an unpleasant truth or changing something about what you are doing. Achieving any win starts with asking yourself questions.

Bring This Trait to Life
Take some time to reflect. It can be a few minutes over coffee, or it can be a more in-depth period of time, like a personal retreat. The point is to give yourself some space and time to reveal what is important for you. Here are a few sample questions to think about in relation to your personal and/or professional life:

▲ Am I happy with my current circumstances?
▲ What is working? What isn't?
▲ How would I define a win in my life?
▲ What am I willing to do about it?

After answering your questions honestly, consider what you might change or continue to do.

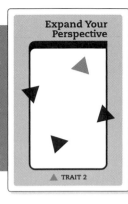

Expand Your Perspective

▲ TRAIT 2

TRAIT 2:

Expand Your Perspective

KEY CONCEPT
By looking at circumstances differently, you access new realms of possibility for yourself.

MARK: *In the weeks following the Pan Pacifics where Jeff broke the world record and shattered my dreams, I was invited to a wedding. Michelle Cameron, an Olympic synchronized swimming champion, was getting married to Al Coulter, an Olympic volleyball player. With ten months to go before the Olympics and absolutely no idea how I was ever going to overcome this disastrous situation, I wasn't exactly in a celebrating mood. The idea of having hundreds of people from the world of sport ask me "How are things going?" was more than I could bear. I was dreading it. Before I even arrived, I had made up my mind that I wasn't going to have a good time.*

DEBBIE: Michelle had been one of my athletes, and it was at the wedding reception that I ran into Mark again. We hadn't really been in contact with each other since our time together in Perth, and when I saw him, I could tell immediately that something wasn't right. Mark is usually very enthusiastic and positive, but just from the way he said hello, I knew he

17

wasn't himself. I asked him if everything was okay, and he very honestly said no. He told me briefly about his setback, but he realized that it wasn't really the time or the place to get into it. So we set a date for lunch the following week.

MARK: *Seeing Debbie helped me get out of my funk for a few moments that night. And despite my earlier misgivings, there was something about being at this wedding that was actually inspiring. Looking at Michelle, a gold medalist in the Seoul Olympics, helped me to see that it was actually possible to be from Calgary, where I was living, and be a champion. If she could do it, maybe I could, too.*

One area where I was particularly weak was my underwater technique, which is essential to the start and the turns, accounting for about 30 percent of every race. Because Debbie was a synchronized swimming coach, she was an expert in this area, and I thought she could give me some tips about techniques and training. I really had no idea of the significance of the partnership and what was about to happen.

DEBBIE: The first thing that struck me about Mark when we met for that unforgettable lunch was the fact that this guy wanted to win more than anyone I had seen. Listening to him talk, I could see there were many opportunities for improving his training. Things like underwater kicking, breath holding, and transitioning out of starts and turns had not been explored much. I started to see the possibility of what could happen if I helped him with these areas. I knew it wouldn't be easy, but I remember thinking to myself, "This guy wants it so badly. He's got the ability. And he seems willing to do whatever it will take." As a coach, that combination was irresistible. I got really excited thinking that he could actually do this. And when I shared that thought with Mark, he welled up with emotion.

I don't think either of us had expected the energy that would be created when we came together. When Mark saw that I genuinely thought he could do it, he completely opened to the idea that he could make it happen for himself. As our lunch went into the three-hour mark, we could both clearly see the possibility. And once we saw it, there was no going back.

TO BE A CHAMPION:
1. Notice What You Notice
2. Be Open to See Things Differently
3. Gain Insight by Increasing Perspective

ACHIEVERS

1. Notice What You Notice

It is human nature to have selective awareness. We set ourselves up and are set up to notice certain things. Think about it. When you buy a new red car, what happens? You notice more red cars. What happens when you are pregnant? You suddenly notice other pregnant women at every turn. When you are trying to stop smoking, what do you see? People smoking everywhere! It is natural that our attention is drawn to what we are most conscious of. Without even realizing it, we go through the day seeing, hearing, feeling only what we have set ourselves up to see, hear, and feel, usually to the exclusion of everything else. If we wake up in a bad mood, for example, all day long we tend to pay attention to events and people that reinforce how bad things are. Sometimes the biggest factor holding us back can be the way we see things. Ask yourself: In only noticing certain things, what might I be missing?

2. Be Open to See Things Differently

A narrow perspective limits us in terms of what is possible and how we choose to get there. Realize that there is always more than one way to do things, and there are often many different possibilities when we are ready to see them. When you open yourself to see situations differently, there is less chance of getting stuck, feeling frustrated and hopeless, or going down the wrong path because you can see only one solution. You might decide to do the same thing over again, but that decision comes after considering numerous possibilities. Increased perspective helps break the pattern of history repeating itself or making the same mistakes over and over again. It challenges your natural inclination toward having "selective aware-ness," and enhances your ability to explore various possibilities and ideas.

Expanding your perspective opens whole new realms of possibility, as Mary quickly discovered.

DEBBIE: Mary was incredibly smart, but she came to the world of coaching from the perspective of a chartered accountant. In her mind, unless something was perfect, it was wrong. From her point of view, everything was an absolute: 2 + 2 = 4. That was it. There was no room for deviation from this. But what that meant for the athletes she worked with was that something that was 98 percent right was seen as failure, because it had to be either exactly right or it was wrong. Her swimmers were getting completely discouraged. I challenged Mary to make only positive comments about what she liked for two weeks. "But how are we going to get better if we aren't fixing what is wrong?" she argued. "Just try it," I responded. Two days later she called me. "It's like a miracle," she stated. "Not only am I realizing that we are good at so many things, we are actually fixing what isn't working as I focus on what is." Her limited perspective was impacting those around her in the worst way imaginable. Shifting her perspective changed that.

3. Gain Insight by Increasing Perspective

There is a strange irony here. The more open you are to possibility, the clearer you eventually become about the things that really matter. The whole point of expanding your perspective is to ultimately gain insight into where you need to focus your attention. There is a correlation between staying open to new ideas and possibilities, and being even more focused on what you need to do. The fundamental skill that this trait develops is your power of observation. Your ability to notice more of what is going on around you allows you to constantly stay open to all kinds of possibility. Ultimately, through this openness, you gain insight into what is important in any given situation.

MARK: *My debut performance at the Seoul Olympics was a complete disaster. I was so nervous I swam much too fast for the first part of the race, and although in world record time, could not sustain it. I faded badly and ended 20-something in the rankings. My next race was better, but still way off of my personal best; where I had been expected to win a medal,*

I came a disappointing fifth. In my mind, the Olympics were a huge disappointment even though I still had one more event left, the 4 × 100 m medley relay.

On the morning of the race, one of my teammates, Victor Davis, said he thought we could win a medal if we all did what we were capable of. I was so disappointed from earlier swims that I couldn't believe what he was saying. I was completely closed to the idea. A couple of hours before the race, Victor confronted me. "What did you dream of when you were a kid?" he asked. "To win a medal at the Olympics," I replied. "Well, you better wake up, because this is your chance. But it's up to you," he grunted.

Victor forced me to consider the possibility. Of course I wanted to win a medal, but my perspective had gotten narrower and narrower as the Games progressed. Victor's comment was like a wake-up call that helped me see the bigger picture again, and then focus on what I needed to do. We would shock everyone by taking the silver medal in the final swimming race on the Olympic program.

ACHIEVERS

ACHIEVERS

▲ TRAIT 2 REVIEW: Expand Your Perspective

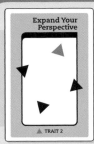

Expand Your Perspective

▲ TRAIT 2

TO BE A CHAMPION:
1. Notice What You Notice
2. Be Open to See Things Differently
3. Gain Insight by Increasing Perspective

KEY CONCEPT
By looking at circumstances differently, you access new realms of possibility for yourself.

REALITY CHECK!
Sometimes the biggest factor holding you back is the way you see things. You limit your perspective about what is and isn't possible. Expanding your perspective means staying open to hear new ideas and see things you have never seen before. The more you notice, the more perspective you gain. You discover new possibilities in terms of what you can achieve and different ways of making them happen.

Bring This Trait to Life
Shake things up a bit. For one day or one week, take something out of your life that you might take for granted, and see how your perspective changes. Try going a day without eating any meat, or not driving your car, or not having that cup of coffee in the morning. What other meal options might be on the menu? What are other ways of getting around without your car? What might you substitute for the coffee? Taking away something that you automatically include in your routine forces you to consider other possibilities, to see things differently, and will give you perspective on what you might have taken for granted before.

Make a Plan

▲ TRAIT 3

TRAIT 3:
Make a Plan

KEY CONCEPT
By laying the foundation for focused action, you create
a clear path to take you to your desired win.

DEBBIE: Following our initial lunch meeting, both Mark and I looked to the future with great excitement. But, I knew that if this partnership was really going to work, we needed a solid plan to clearly map out exactly what we would have to do to make this dream a reality. Planning is not the most exciting activity. In fact, with all of the details that we needed to consider, it was quite tedious. But this was a fundamental step in harnessing all of those good feelings that we shared into something more concrete.

MARK: *As an athlete, I had enjoyed slightly better results year after year, which is why I had never even thought about creating a plan for myself. As long as I was improving, why should I bother planning? I just kind of chugged along, letting one year follow the next, content to let life happen.*

When I found myself in the place where I had to make seven years' improvement in less than ten months, everything changed. I couldn't rely on just letting life unfold as it had in the past. I needed my own specific plan to get myself to that higher level of performance. That started by clearly identifying what my goal was, and then charting a detailed path to get there.

It felt very strange to actually write down my objective for the first time: I wanted to become an Olympic champion. But that seemed such a stretch from anything that I had done in the past that it kind of freaked me out to see it on paper. But, at the same time, it made me completely commit to reaching my goal. The planning process was like a roller coaster ride. It was exciting to imagine the end result, depressing and scary to see where I was with only months to go, but hopeful as we started to identify all of the different things we were going to do to make it happen.

DEBBIE: Mark told me, "I want to do everything possible to be my best this year." That gave us a starting point to honestly assess all that needed to be done. I knew that as long as he had done everything possible, he could live with whatever the result proved to be. That was our guide. The basic core element of swimming training was already taken care of. We looked at all of the different ways we could support that to make him better. There was technical work, strength, endurance, breath holding, and reaction time training. We broke down each of these into a step-by-step process, month-by-month, week-by-week, day-by-day.

MARK: *In the past, it had always seemed to me that I had all the time in the world to make this happen. I knew that if I didn't win these upcoming Olympics, then it wasn't ever going to happen because I wasn't going to be able to commit yet another four years to this dream. It forced me to plan. As much as I hated it at first, I came to realize how crucial this was. And once I understood how to create a thorough plan, it became something that I have done for myself every single year since.*

TO BE A CHAMPION:
1. Identify Your Win
2. See Where You Are Now
3. Identify What Needs to Be Done

ACHIEVERS

1. Identify Your Win

We know that this is not the sexiest of our traits, but it is hugely important that you master it nonetheless. Planning is a fundamental skill that often gets overlooked. We know many people who refuse to plan and end up doing things that are completely ineffective, finding themselves going in endless circles. The time you invest in planning will save countless hours of unfocused execution, creating an enormous return on investment. It is always good to go through the planning process. Let us take you through ours.

The first action is to determine **SPECIFICALLY** what it is you want to achieve. Every great plan begins with the end in mind, or at least an idea of what the end will be. Take the time to reflect and ask yourself powerful questions that help you reveal what it is you would like to achieve. We cannot stress enough how important this seemingly simple step is. It has a couple of important consequences: First, when you write down your goal, it becomes real. The act of writing it down strengthens your commitment. Second, when you put your goal on paper, it becomes the ultimate milestone against which everything else gets measured. When you write down specifically what it is you want to achieve, your intention starts to align with your thoughts and actions. Big or small, long term or short, this simple step is the first part of the planning process.

2. See Where You Are Now

The next step is straightforward, but it comes with its own challenges. Before you can get where you want to go, you need to look **HONESTLY** at where you are right now—in relation to that specific goal. Build on the skills you developed in Trait 1: Ask Yourself Questions. Be brutally honest about where you find yourself. The truth needs to be revealed so you can best map your way to where you want to go.

There is no judgement here—no "good" or "bad"—just the facts. Without the facts, you cannot know your starting point. Here is where you must take score. Be willing to ask yourself some tough questions:

▲ How realistic is my goal given where I am?

▲ Do I have the resources required to reach my goal?

▲ Where are the gaps?

This step lays the foundation for focused action to happen. You have your starting point, an honest idea of where you are, and you also have your finish line, your specific goal. Now you get to find the way there!

DEBBIE: Every year, I faced the same situation with an athlete who couldn't understand why she didn't make the national team. Her downfall was her inability to be honest about her own talent and skill level. She always thought she was better than she actually was. In her mind, her poor results were always the fault of the judges or the coaches. She could never look at the real work she needed to do because she thought she was further ahead than she really was. This unrealistic view, and her subsequent inability to identify the actions she would need to take to be better, kept her back from ever achieving her win.

3. Identify What Needs to Be Done

Now that you've been brutally honest about where you are and know specifically where you want to go, two things have to happen. First, you need to **OUTLINE** the various actions that have to be taken, and the benchmarks that need to be reached along the way. Benchmarks are simply smaller goals that need to be identified and reached en route to achieving the overall objective. Planning is part vision—seeing what you want—but it leads to action, which is why this step is so important. To create your outline, follow these steps:

▲ Identify your benchmarks—the smaller achievements—that need to be reached along the way to your overall objective.

▲ Make a prioritized, step-by-step action list so you know where to start. What action needs to happen first? Then next? And so on...

▲ Longer term, consider what needs to happen to continue to bridge the gaps and update your action list.

Secondly, you need to attach a **TIMELINE** for every action and benchmark. This is important for two reasons: It creates a sense of urgency by showing you there is not an infinite amount of time to get there. It also makes sure you are being realistic and are giving yourself enough time to do all that is needed to achieve your goal.

Following these simple steps ensures that you reach your objectives. Taking the time to do the planning process gives you something on paper that will act as a guide as you go forward. With this trait, you've given yourself the best SHOT possible to lay the blueprint to achieve whatever it is your heart desires. In summary:

S: Write down **SPECIFICALLY** what you want to achieve.

H: **HONESTLY** assess where you are.

O: **OUTLINE** the actions that have to be taken, and the benchmarks that need to be reached.

T: Attach a prioritized **TIMELINE** to each action and benchmark.

DEBBIE: In order for Carolyn Waldo to become an Olympic champion, we decided that she needed to start her routine with the longest underwater sequence that had ever been done in the history of synchronized swimming. Where most athletes would stay under for 30 seconds, we were going for one minute. On top of that, we wanted to keep a high degree of difficulty right through to the end of her performance. We were clear about what we wanted to achieve, and we built a plan around that. We looked at all of the different types of training that would be needed so she could hold her breath longer than anyone else had in the world, and maintain her strength and power for the rest of her routine. Working backwards, we designed a two-year detailed program so that Carolyn would make it look easy once we got to the Olympics in Seoul.

For a year and nine months, we worked diligently behind the scenes, following the plan that we had made for ourselves. With three months to go before the actual Games, we had a pre-Olympic competition where we unveiled the routine for the first time. The defending Olympic champion, Tracie Ruiz-Conforto from the United States, was our main rival.

ACHIEVERS

At this competition, she saw how long Carolyn's underwater sequence was, and because of this, she went home and changed her routine, arriving at the Olympics with an even longer first underwater segment than Carolyn.

I felt sick the first time I saw Tracie practice the opening of her routine at the Olympics. That was, until she came up for air and passed out in the water. She literally couldn't finish. I thought to myself, "Wow. Good thing we spent two years making ours work!" We had been clear about what we wanted, and had worked for years to make it happen.

And it had paid off. Carolyn went on to win the Olympic gold medal.

Tracie made it through the routine, but had to settle for second. Taking the time to plan helped Carolyn and me over the two years to do the right thing at the right time in order to get the results we wanted. Tracie fell into a trap that is not uncommon: too often, people don't allow themselves enough time to get where they want to go. They decide to make a plan much too late for it to be effective. Ultimately, in my case, planning made the difference between winning or not.

ACHIEVERS

▲ TRAIT 3 REVIEW: Make a Plan

TO BE A CHAMPION:
1. Identify Your Win
2. See Where You Are Now
3. Identify What Needs to Be Done

ACHIEVERS

KEY CONCEPT

By laying the foundation for focused action, you create a clear path to take you to your desired win.

REALITY CHECK!

Sometimes you might get overwhelmed thinking about all that needs to be done, so you never actually sit down and organize your thoughts, taking the time to make a plan. At other times, you might be so gung ho that you don't want to take the time to stop and think, you just want to go. In either case, do yourself a favour and take the time to make a plan. It will help you clarify exactly what needs to be done, and help you set a timeline for when you need to do it. The fundamental skill of planning makes your actions focused and meaningful.

Bring This Trait to Life

Use the SHOT process: Let's imagine your goal is to give up caffeine.

S: I want to give up caffeine.

H: I drink six cups of caffeinated coffee a day.

O: Introduce decaffeinated coffee. Buy Tylenol for headaches. Warn friends I might be cranky.

T: Week one: Go from six cups a day to three. Week two: Have half decaf/half caffeine. Week three: Only drink decaffeinated coffee.

Try it with your own goal and see how it works.

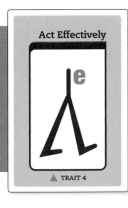

Act Effectively

▲ TRAIT 4

TRAIT 4:
Act Effectively

KEY CONCEPT
By aligning your day-to-day actions with your objectives,
you ensure that what you are doing will keep you on track.

MARK: *Debbie and I met a few times following our decision to work together in order to carefully plan out what we needed to do. It was on a Thursday morning, two weeks after the famous lunch, when we actually made it to the pool for the first time. Finally, we were going to get down to work. We had mapped out what we had to do, but the minute we went to implement the plan, we ran into our first problem.*

DEBBIE: When Mark got in and showed me his underwater kicking technique and ability to hold his breath, I saw immediately that we had an even bigger challenge than we had realized. He was much weaker than I had thought he would be. Because Mark was a world-class swimmer, I had assumed that he had a basic foundation of underwater technical skill. He didn't. If this was going to work, we had to completely step away from the plan that we had just made and figure out a new starting point. In this case, it meant taking several steps backwards to get Mark to a place where he could be effective. It was a good wake-up call early in the process. This experience showed us that even though the plan was still hugely important, it was simply a guide that was only as good as our ability to adjust to reality. It was useful to have a detailed plan, but we had to pay close attention to what was working and what wasn't.

MARK: *For me, this was completely heartbreaking. I was already overwhelmed by how much we had to do. Then, to have a setback before I had even really started was brutal. But I learned something invaluable from the experience. In the past, my coaches had often asked me to do things but I was never given a clear explanation about why I was doing them. I felt like sometimes we were doing things just for the sake of it, and when I asked, "Why are we doing this," the response would be "Because." This time I knew we had to change things, and Debbie was great at explaining why. I understood that what we were doing was going to help us be more effective in the long run, even though it seemed at first as if we were taking several steps backwards.*

DEBBIE: I am not going to downplay how much there was to do, because there was a lot. I knew that just as we hadn't started at the right place, there would be other surprises along the way that we could not foresee. The important thing was to make the best decisions based on the feedback we were getting from Mark's results in training and competition. Until we actually started, we didn't have anything to respond to. If we had tried to barrel through and stay with the original plan, then Mark would not have made it.

We had to go back to a more rudimentary level that gave Mark the foundation to build his underwater technique properly. This raised not only his skill set, but also his confidence. It was amazing to see how quickly Mark started to improve once he fixed his technique and had some success. It reinforced his confidence and we caught up to our original schedule much faster than we thought we would.

TO BE A CHAMPION:
1. Just Get Started
2. Evaluate Your Actions
3. Make Effective Decisions

1. Just Get Started

Making a plan is a fundamental part of achievement, but without this trait, Act Effectively, the best laid plan in the world is for nothing. It is one thing to think you know what to do—to have a plan written down on paper. It is another to execute it effectively and actually do what needs to be done in any given circumstance to take you closer to your goal. This is where the rubber hits the road. Simple, right?

This is where so many people run into challenges. As exciting as your goal may be, there will always be distractions and endless excuses why you can put off getting to the work. Procrastination is the enemy of progress. No matter how daunting the road ahead may seem—just start! Look at your outline of prioritized actions that you made in Trait 3: Make a Plan. Take the first one. Do it.

Until you actually begin, you don't have anything to react to. It is imagination versus reality. The only way to turn your goal into something real is to take action. Get to it!

2. Evaluate Your Actions

Acting effectively is about putting your plan into action and then finding what works. The plan acts as a guide—to be followed when everything goes well, and finding an alternative when it doesn't. A common mistake is that people get so stuck in delivering the plan, they forget to pay attention to whether things are working or not. Remember, things rarely go as planned. Your ability to evaluate what you are doing becomes extremely important here. Pay attention to the results you are getting.

To help you evaluate whether you are on the right track, here are some fundamental questions you need to ask yourself on a regular basis:

- ▲ Is what I am doing leading me to where I want to go?
- ▲ What will happen if I keep doing what I am doing?
- ▲ Is there a better way to do what I am doing?
- ▲ Are my actions aligned with my goal?

DEBBIE: One of my main competitors once shared some of her coaching ideas with me, specifically how she was going to integrate complex scientific concepts that I had never even heard of into her training regimen. By the time she finished explaining what she was going to do, I thought to myself, "Oh man, she is incredible. We are going to be toast when we compete against her!" But when I saw her team swim three months later, I had never before seen such a disconnect between a plan and its execution. Her swimmers lacked all of the major elements they needed to succeed. If there had been a gold medal for planning, she would have won. But in terms of delivering the goods, she completely missed the mark. Maybe she worked long days, maybe she worked hard, but her team certainly didn't do what they needed to do in order to win—act effectively.

It is one thing to have a plan, but if you aren't able to implement it effectively, you are missing the point. It is not just about execution, it is also about making sure you have planned properly. If you haven't, you might need to change the plan.

3. Make Effective Decisions

Over time, you will see that planning and action merge through effective decision making. Remember that the plan is the road map, but it shouldn't hold you prisoner. With each action you take, you get new information that helps you determine whether you are on track or not. The onus is on you to make the best decision possible in terms of your next step as a result of evaluating your actions. The secret is to be flexible, seize opportunities, and be nimble in order to make good decisions that align your actions with your goal. Trust yourself to do what is right in specific situations, even if it is different from what you had planned. Ultimately, acting effectively is doing what works!

One note of caution: Don't confuse busyness with effectiveness. Continually ask yourself if what you are doing is taking you closer to your goal. If it is, keep doing it. If not, figure out why not and change it until you find something that works. It is up to you to keep finding the way.

MARK: *When I was a young swimmer just coming onto the national team, we went to train in the mountains of France for three weeks, thinking we were getting a competitive edge. Altitude training was highly regarded, but because of its intense nature, it was also rather controversial. Swimming in thin air had its benefits, like increasing the red blood cell count, which helped endurance, but we had to be carefully monitored to avoid severe overtraining. With a carefully mapped-out plan, off we went.*

The problem was that we based our plan on those of the East German and Chinese teams, before it had been officially confirmed that they had used drugs to help them recover in training. As each day went by, and we followed their incredible regimen but without the artificial aids, we began, one by one, to slowly drop off from sheer exhaustion. In spite of what was happening, we decided to stick to the plan. As the seriousness of the situation became apparent, we were too slow to change and the damage had been done. Physiologically, we had depleted our reserves to the point of no return. For many of us, it took two years to fully recover from the overtraining that we had done. Our outcome was exactly the opposite of what had been intended.

ACHIEVERS

▲ TRAIT 4 REVIEW: Act Effectively

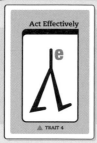

TO BE A CHAMPION:

1. Just Get Started
2. Evaluate Your Actions
3. Make Effective Decisions

KEY CONCEPT

By aligning your day-to-day actions with your objectives, you ensure that what you are doing will keep you on track.

REALITY CHECK!

There is only so much time, resources, and energy in a day, so we have to maximize those by acting effectively. Planning and action merge through effective decision making. Ask yourself, "Is what I am doing working or not?" If it isn't working, make a change. It is pretty simple. Where you might fall short is when you forget to check in with the plan and see if your actions are taking you where you want to go.

The plan only gives you an idea of what to do. Being effective means the onus is on you to constantly evaluate whether your actions are on track.

Bring This Trait to Life

To stay on a winning track, check in with this checklist.

Ask yourself these questions at the end of the day:
- ▲ Did today really matter?
- ▲ Did my actions today move me closer to my goal?
- ▲ Did I learn something that moved me forward?
- ▲ Were my actions as efficient and effective as they could be? If they weren't, what can I do differently tomorrow to get back on the winning track?

Go the
Distance

▲ TRAIT 5

TRAIT 5:
Go the Distance

On the way to achieving your desired win, you must be
willing to persist through tough times and periods
of hard work.

MARK: *From the very beginning of our work together, Debbie and I based our process on three fundamental steps. Step one was to focus intensely on skill training, such as underwater kick, in isolation. Step two was to integrate those new skills back into my regular swimming regime. The final step was to bring those skills to competition, where there was a much higher degree of pressure. Making it through each phase proved to be harder than I imagined. The first time I used my improved underwater kicking technique in a race, I was too good! We were only allowed to stay under for 15 meters, and my kick was so strong that I went 18. I was disqualified, and faced yet another setback.*

DEBBIE: It was tough, because we were trying so hard to prove to all of the doubters that what we were doing was working. Sometimes when you start something new, there is a little thought that says, "Okay, this is going to be magic. We'll show all those people who don't believe." And then it hurts like hell when you actually prove them temporarily right. We really had to find the positive advances and believe in what we were doing. Yes, Mark went too far off the start in the competition. But it was because his underwater technique was so much better, which meant we were on the right track. It took some time to make the many adjustments we needed to make, but Mark never gave up, even though most people around him remained sceptical.

MARK: *Not giving up took on a whole new meaning later that year. For three weeks over Christmas, my team traveled to Australia for a training camp. Because the Olympics were in an outdoor pool in Barcelona and our pool at home was indoors, we needed to invest some time training under the sun to get used to it. It was there that we met a coach who specialized in endurance training. I had known periods of long, hard work before, but I had never before experienced anything like this. We did something called a heart rate set. Essentially, we were asked to get our heart rates to 180 beats per minute (bpm), and then keep it there for an hour. In a typically challenging set, my heart rate might peak at 180 to 200 bpm, but for much, much shorter periods of time. Keeping it at 180 bpm for an hour was unheard of, even for elite athletes. It was the most intense session I had ever been asked to do in my life.*

In order to get the most out of the set, not only did I do the long, painful swimming sessions, I also integrated the underwater technique that I had been doing with Debbie into the workout. It was the combination of the hour-long intense set, working on the underwater kick off the start and turn on every single length, and learning to cope with the paralyzing buildup of lactic acid in my system that compounded the results of this set for me.

DEBBIE: Part of the focus that year was to get through the monotonous drudgery of the day-to-day training. This is where you get to show who you are and what you are made of, and it is where, unfortunately, so many people give up. Were there times when it wasn't pretty? Absolutely there were, especially during some of those long, dark Alberta winter days. But getting through those times was a fundamental part of the process.

MARK: *Something that helped me make it through was that we constantly celebrated the little improvements along the way. When I first swam* *underwater for 15 meters straight, we cheered. Over time, I saw that we were making major gains. At the Winter Nationals, I broke the Canadian record. I knew there was no guarantee that I was going to eventually win my race at the Olympics, so we didn't wait to enjoy that moment in the future; we made sure to celebrate the process—the small victories—along the way. It was these moments that made the hard work tolerable.*

TO BE A CHAMPION
1. Never Give Up
2. Pay Attention to the Details
3. Enjoy the Journey

ACHIEVERS

1. Never Give Up

Going the distance means you endure the drudgery, you overcome the challenges, and you put in the time. Where planning provides the road map, it is the long-term commitment of acting effectively *over time* that ultimately turns possibility into results. The daily grind, the slog, the routine is the part that sometimes isn't much fun. This is the trait that asks you to persevere, go the extra mile, and rise above and beyond what you've asked of yourself before. It tests your commitment.

You might look for shortcuts, hoping for an easier way. When you take the easy alternative, often one of two things happens. You hit a roadblock and drastically reduce your expectations, settling for something less. Or, you give up entirely, thinking you will try something else that is easier. No matter what you undertake, there is no avoiding the hard work if you want to be successful.

2. Pay Attention to the Details

Woody Allen famously said that 80 percent of success is showing up, but going the distance isn't just about showing up, going on autopilot, and putting in long hours simply for the sake of it. It is about being focused and doing the thousands of little things that need to be done well along the way. These accumulate to get you where you want to go.

The traits in this book work together. It is the combination of working effectively (Trait 4) over a period of time (Trait 5) that creates a trajectory that takes you from where you are to where you want to be. Often, the difference between winning and losing is miniscule. For example, in many sports, the difference can be measured in thousands of a second. The point here is not to get sloppy. Don't rush things. Pay attention to the details and make them count. Fundamentally, it is effective action and doing the long, hard work over time where results start to get compounded and you ensure that you are doing everything possible to make your win come to life.

3. Enjoy the Journey

Ultimately, you want to accomplish what it is you set out to achieve. The reality is there is no guarantee that you will reach every goal every time. This is why it is so important to enjoy the process along the way. Celebrate progress and small gains. Recognize effort. Take time to laugh. These are the things that will keep you going. Surprisingly, they are also the moments that stand out years later. When you get together with people and reflect, don't you often reminisce about the day-to-day challenges you overcame together? The win was great, but often the journey was even better.

MARK: *In the late 1980s, I was part of a small group of athletes who were let inside the Soviet Union to train with the Russians. I learned some important things there. As much drudgery as there was—for three weeks we ate the same meals, shared limited bathrooms, and endured a hard physical routine—we also had periods of rest, recovery, and fun built in. Who knew it would be the Russians who would teach me to find enjoyment in training? In the middle of the afternoon swimming session, hot tea with honey and biscuits would arrive. We would all finish the set we were doing and take a break together. I came to love these times. The snack was much needed food energy, but it was also a moment to joke around and laugh with each other with limited language skills, hand signals, and body language. It was where the friendships were built. I left Russia knowing that I had put all of this effort into something, and that regardless of what happened in the future, it had been a meaningful experience that I could look back on and fondly remember. Times like those taught me what it meant to enjoy the process while going the distance.*

ACHIEVERS

ACHIEVERS

▲ TRAIT 5 REVIEW: Go the Distance

TO BE A CHAMPION:
1. Never Give Up
2. Pay Attention to the Details
3. Enjoy the Journey

KEY CONCEPT
On the way to achieving your desired win, you must be willing to persist through tough times and periods of hard work.

REALITY CHECK!
At first it is easy to be excited about tackling a new challenge. But as time wears on and fatigue, frustration, disappointment, and stress—reality—all start to appear, it becomes even more important not to give up. Besides, more often than not, it is the insight gained about yourself along the way that you take forward. Results come and go, but the process stays with you forever. It is the capacity to persevere, to overcome the odds and obstacles, that makes the journey so rewarding.

Bring This Trait to Life
We invite you to take the 21-day challenge. The only way to go the distance is with time, so this fun exercise asks you to commit. Choose something that you know you will need to do to reach one of your objectives, something you have been putting off for whatever reason. It might be getting in shape. It might be organizing a neglected room in your house. You get the idea. Commit to doing something about that for the next 21 days in a row. Take a calendar and mark each day that you take action. It could be five minutes a day; it could be a couple of hours. The choice is yours. The point here is to be a champion and go the distance. Watch the calendar numbers climb to 21, and pay attention to how your efforts accumulate.

Be Innovative

▲ TRAIT 6

Be Innovative

KEY CONCEPT
By challenging yourself to tap into new ideas, you find
unique solutions to move forward.

DEBBIE: It had taken the crisis of the Pan Pacific Games to bring Mark
and me together. We had been on the same pool deck hundreds of times,
Mark coming to watch my athletes train, and me to see him compete,
but we had never before made the connection that we could benefit from
working together. Sometimes, innovation is like that—it is just connecting
ideas, experiences, or knowledge in a way that has never been done before.
Simply by working together that year, Mark and I were being innovative.

MARK: *There wasn't just a single moment of being innovative that stands
out from that time. It was more like a creative mindset that took over
that year, eventually becoming a way of being that enabled us to generate
many ideas and take actions that were totally innovative. That outlook
kept building on itself throughout the year to find solutions to problems
as they arose.*

DEBBIE: When we realized that we needed to strengthen Mark's legs to
support the technical work we were doing, there was no way to simulate

43

that specific training in the weight room. So what did we do? We brought the weights right into the water. I tied a 25-pound weight onto a piece of tubing, and then tied that around Mark's waist. He sank like a stone. The challenge was to push off from the bottom of the pool and kick vertically to the surface, the goal being to get his chest out of the water. The first time we tried it, I thought I was going to have to get the lifeguard to rescue him. Mark could barely break the surface of the water with his mouth, let alone get his chest out. But, eventually, he got it. It was simply a matter of finding better ways of doing things in order to achieve the objective.

MARK: *I was in Vancouver for a competition three months before Barcelona. A couple of people I was staying with decided to go and see if they could get tickets to the U2 concert that night. Normally, I wouldn't have gone because I was competing the next day, but one of my friends noted that the stadium held approximately 12,000 people. Something clicked. That was the size of the expected crowd for the final of the 100-meter backstroke at the Olympics. One of my challenges that year was to do something to prepare myself for the energy that those thousands of people would create. I had been to an Olympics before in Seoul, and had been overwhelmed by the enormity of everything. I thought this would be a great way to get over that and feel more comfortable. That night, every time Bono introduced a song and the huge mass of people roared, I took in that energy, thinking not about the upcoming song, but pretending that I was standing on the starting blocks looking out at the crowd at the Olympics. I had never done anything like this before. New thinking led to innovative solutions that ultimately strengthened my confidence.*

Be Innovative

▲ TRAIT 6

TO BE A CHAMPION:
1. Tap Into Your Experience
2. Generate New Ideas
3. Have the Courage to Take Risks

1. Tap Into Your Experience

It is easy to fall into the trap of thinking that innovation requires some kind of Eureka moment that changes the world. Sometimes it does happen like that, but more often it is much simpler. And it starts with you.

Many of us underestimate ourselves and all the experience, skills, and knowledge that have made us who we are. You take what you know for granted. Think about it. There is no one else in the entire world exactly like you. Honour that by acknowledging that your life experience is valuable. Use it to explore ideas, imagine possibilities, and find solutions to challenges as they arise. *You* are the starting point for innovation.

2. Generate New Ideas

Innovation is like a blank slate in that anything can happen as long as you allow yourself to go there. All that is required is to constantly generate ideas *without* editing them. Let your experience guide your imagination and stay open to seeing and hearing new ideas around you. The more ideas you can generate, the greater the possibility that you will find a solution that you might not have known before. It is the right combination of ideas *applied* to a particular challenge that *leads to* an innovative solution. Innovation simply asks you to make connections that you might never have made before.

MARK: *Going into the Olympics can be intimidating. Before the Barcelona Games, in the final days before leaving North America for Europe, Debbie was asked to work with a group of female athletes, specifically to help them build their confidence. Her challenge was to help the women learn to deal with those feelings that are potentially overwhelming, feelings that can come when you find yourself surrounded by the best athletes in the world. Instead of doing a boring workshop in a hotel room, she decided to use the environment around her in a unique way. Since she and the athletes were training in Los Angeles, what could be better for practicing being confident than Beverly Hills?*

It turned out to be the perfect training ground for creating the confidence they would need when they would be surrounded by the best of the best. Five of them crammed into a cheap little car that Debbie rented, and off they went to Rodeo Drive. The whole idea was to look confident even if they didn't necessarily feel it, because they might need that skill when arriving at the Games. None of them felt very comfortable buzzing to be let in to the ultra exclusive shops, or asking to see a piece of jewellery worth hundreds of thousands of dollars. It was absolutely intimidating! But that was exactly the situation Debbie was looking for. It gave the athletes the chance to do something out of their comfort zone. An innovative solution gave them a fun experience that helped them overcome the feelings of insecurity just as they might have in the Olympic environment. In fact, when they got to Barcelona, they couldn't stop smiling as the stress mounted, thinking of what they had done on Rodeo Drive.

3. Have the Courage to Take Risks

Making mistakes is stigmatized in our society. It kicks the courage out of us to try new things. Have the strength to act on the unknown—the innovative idea. This trait isn't about creating just for the sake of it. It is about taking calculated risks, not stupid ones. Find the right idea that can be applied to the right situation, and then act on it. Innovation enables us to find new ways forward. We believe that there is no failure, only feedback. If your idea wasn't quite as brilliant as you thought it would be, have the courage to try something else.

DEBBIE: I was three months out from the Olympics and I knew our synchronized swimming team had a problem. Our routine was great—technically excellent with a high degree of difficulty—but it was missing a punch at the end. We had set the routine to the music from Spartacus, which was serious and compelling, but it wasn't going to get the crowd on their feet. In order to win, it became clear that we would have to make some drastic changes. Initially, we tried working harder; then we tried to change the choreography. When neither worked, we saw we had to take a risky and scary step and change an entire sequence of music. The great innovative breakthrough came from mixing two completely different styles of music to get the effect we were looking for. We went from the serious Spartacus theme straight into Offenbach's popular theme, the Can-Can. To some this might have been like mixing oil and water, but to us it was a risk that made sense. It paid off, and we ended up winning the Olympic gold medal.

▲ TRAIT 6 REVIEW: Be Innovative

TO BE A CHAMPION:

1. Tap Into Your Experience
2. Generate New Ideas
3. Have the Courage to Take Risks

KEY CONCEPT

By challenging yourself to tap into new ideas, you find unique solutions to move forward.

REALITY CHECK!

It can be too easy to do things the same way we have always done them, finding ourselves getting stuck at the same place. But, with innovation, that doesn't need to happen. Are you open to seeing things you have never seen before, and then acting on them? Just using your experience, skills, and knowledge to find a creative solution to a problem that arises can be an innovation. Keep an open mind and see it work for you.

Bring This Trait to Life

Take a problem or challenge that you are currently facing, and for 10 minutes generate a list of solutions. Don't overthink, just write. Be as imaginative and out there as you can. The point here is to generate as many ideas as possible. Make them crazy, seemingly impossible, whatever. Now, let all the ideas float around in your head for a day or two. Pay attention to what new connections you might make, and what solution might emerge.

ACHIEVERS

Utilize Power
of Thought

▲ TRAIT 7

TRAIT 7:
Utilize Power of Thought

KEY CONCEPT
By mastering your thoughts, you have a much greater chance of accessing your full potential.

DEBBIE: After a couple of months of working together, I began to notice that although Mark and I were doing some great physical training, we weren't getting the most out of our workouts. Something wasn't right. Having coached many champions before, I could hear from the way Mark was talking that he wasn't *thinking* like a champion. Many times, he just seemed to lack the confidence he would need to be the best in the world. One afternoon after a workout, I asked him pointedly, "Mark, why *can't* you beat Jeff Rouse?" His response was shocking—and enlightening. I was expecting him to say that there was no reason why he couldn't win. Instead, his reply gave us both a huge insight into what was running through his mind.

MARK: *Before I could stop myself, I blurted out about ten different reasons why I didn't think I could do it. To be honest, I didn't even realize that all of these negative thoughts had been there. They had been boiling under the surface, and finally they came into consciousness for me. Over time, these subconscious thoughts had reinforced my belief that I couldn't win* *the Olympics. This thinking was holding me back from being completely engaged, and it was having a negative impact on my physical preparation. Now that I was aware of it, we could do something to change that.*

Whenever we had spoken about winning, that little voice in my head would say, "But you've never won the Olympics or World Championships before. When the big event comes, you have always just missed out. What makes you think you can do it now?" Unveiling this self-talk immediately took away some of its power. Simply facing it gave me confidence. We identified the problem: I needed to change this limited thinking, and for the rest of the year, we made sure my thinking was working for me, not against me.

DEBBIE: Mark really opened up, sharing anything that came to his mind that he thought might be holding him back. With about five months to go before the Barcelona Olympics, Mark told me he was really having a hard time imagining himself winning. Whenever he thought of his backstroke event in the Olympics, he reverted to his experience of the past where he had missed the medal podium. We came up with a plan to change that.

Before my athletes became Olympic champions, we had gone to see the venues and get a feel for the city in which they would compete—Seoul in 1988. It was at a time when the pressure of the Olympics wasn't upon them, and we could have some fun and enjoy the city. It turned out to be a great idea. When we went back for the actual Games, there was a familiarity, and even a bit of recognition, from the Korean public. We thought the same thing would work really well for Mark if he went to Barcelona early.

MARK: *So that was what I did. I went to Barcelona five months before the Games and walked the long rambling boulevards, taking in the energy of the people out in the streets, and completely connected with the city. I went to the Olympic pool, which was still under construction, but imagined myself racing there. It was an incredible experience because from that moment forward, I felt good when I thought about the Olympics. I could visualize myself winning instead of being stuck as an also-ran. Those were the results of the past. When I actually got to the Olympics in July, it was déjà vu. I had already been there in person, and then again hundreds of times in my mind. It gave me a secret competitive edge.*

DEBBIE: Mark and I were doing all of this detailed, thorough work, but it was right before he left Canada for the final ten weeks of training that we really gave our full attention to the mental preparation. A sports psychologist gave Mark a workbook filled with exercises for visualization, affirmation, and script writing. Initially, we ignored it, which just goes to show how easy it is to overlook the mental part of the journey.

One evening when we returned home from dinner, we decided to take a few minutes and look at the workbook. For fun, we just started flipping through it. Mark did one exercise and before you knew it, we were completely engrossed. The Sun was rising as we finished. It would turn out to be one of the most important final details.

MARK: *It started with an affirmations exercise that was in the book. I wrote: "I am fast. I am strong. I am fit. I am gutsy." At first, I thought it was a bit of a joke, but as the powerful words kept coming, I started to get into it. So I kept going. I wrote out a list of the people on the team I would use for support, the challenges I might face, and the solutions or ideas to remember if they arose. The highlight was using words to create a script for my race. "I see myself FOCUSED in the warm-up. I feel GORGEOUS. I am SPECTACULAR. We are called for the race and I feel EXCITED and EMPOWERED. I walk to my lane and SMILE. I am READY. I swim PERFECTLY. I look at the scoreboard and feel MONUMENTAL. I have performed my BEST, EVER. I am PROUD. I have WON." For the next ten weeks, I read and reread the things I had written in this workbook, over and over. I was one of the only swimmers who took it seriously. Ten weeks later, my thoughts came to life.*

Utilize Power of Thought

TRAIT 7

TO BE A CHAMPION:
1. Know What Is Running Through Your Head
2. Understand How Your Thoughts Shape Your Beliefs
3. Use Your Thoughts to Drive Your Actions

1. Know What Is Running Through Your Head

En route to getting what we want, most of us focus on what we have to *do*, and pay very little attention to what we have to *think*. The fundamental learning of this trait is to understand that our actions—what we do and how we do it—are direct products of what we think about all day long. The interesting thing is that most of us don't ever stop to *think about what we think about*. By some estimates, we have 60,000 thoughts a day, most at the subconscious level. Of these thoughts, 80 percent are about ourselves. And approximately two-thirds of these self-centered thoughts are negative in nature. That is over 30,000 negative thoughts a day (or over 20 every minute)! To make matters worse, we tend to have the same thoughts day after day after day. This explains why it can be so hard to get ourselves out of a rut. Don't leave your thinking at the subconscious level. Start to become aware of what is running through your head.

2. Understand How Your Thoughts Shape Your Beliefs

Over time, the repetition of your thoughts turns them into deep-seated beliefs that tell you what you can and cannot do. If you leave your thinking submerged at the subconscious level, this is where you also unwittingly leave your belief for what is possible for yourself. There is an interconnectedness between your thoughts and your beliefs.

How can you become more aware of that connection? There are some key factors that help shape what your belief system ultimately becomes. Through understanding how these factors work, you are more able to use your thoughts to create an empowering belief system.

▲ Self-Talk

Supposedly we talk to ourselves all of the time except for a few seconds an hour. That's a lot of talking, and most of it is happening at the subconscious level. That mental chitchat is called self-talk and it has to go somewhere, and that is likely your belief system. It becomes a self-fulfilling prophecy: If you tell yourself all day long that you are useless, for example, that is often what you become. Start to notice what you are saying to yourself. Ask yourself, "What messages am I reinforcing?"

▲ Your Own Verbal and Non-Verbal Language

Verbally, your thoughts take the form of words. Pay attention to the words you are using in conversation with others and inside your own head. Are those words limiting in nature or are they positive and empowering?

In terms of non-verbal language, your actions (and behavior) convey what you might be thinking. Sometimes actions do speak louder than words. Ask yourself what message you are giving with your body language.

▲ Verbal and Non-Verbal Language of Others

What other people say and do to you can have a profound impact on your own thinking and, ultimately, on your belief system. What they say with their words and actions might sneak in below your level of consciousness and start to play with your thinking, unbeknownst to you. Pay attention! Don't let the negative view of others shape what you believe is possible for yourself.

▲ Interpreting Your Own Unique Experiences

Every experience that you have produces some kind of thought, again often at the subconscious level. Be aware of these thoughts. You don't need to let the past shape the future—unless you want it to. Just because something happened once, or even many times, doesn't mean it has to happen again.

3. Use Your Thoughts to Drive Your Actions

There is a mind–body connection that is so obvious that many of us don't realize its implications. Every thought and belief is connected in some way to our physiology. What we think is literally what we get.

ACHIEVERS

The Thought Cycle

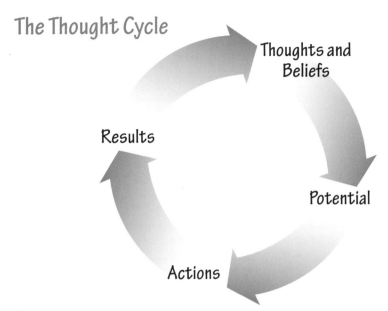

Thoughts and
Beliefs

Results

Potential

Actions

Here is how it works:

The Thought Cycle is simple. Your thoughts and beliefs unlock your potential, influencing directly just how much you can or cannot access. This in turn initiates what actions you take, which then produces a certain result. This result reinforces your thoughts and beliefs, bringing you right back to the beginning of the cycle. The goal is to create an empowering positive Thought Cycle that brings you success. If you are not getting the results you are looking for, you need to do things differently. Sometimes this will mean changing actions—*what you are doing*. Sometimes it means changing your thoughts—*what you are thinking*.

The exciting thing is that you don't have to be at the mercy of your subconscious thoughts. You can develop your thinking to get the kind of results you are looking for.

There are numerous techniques you can master. Here are three to start:

▲ Become More Aware

Acknowledge your thoughts and beliefs, and consider whether they are limiting or empowering. That is often enough to change them. At the very least, becoming more aware of what is running through your head will show what thoughts or actions you might need to change to break a negative cycle.

▲ Take Control of Words

You can train your thoughts by consciously deciding what words you use. Just as repeating an action over time makes it second nature—covering your mouth when you yawn is an example—so, too, can you repeat your thoughts to become second nature and empowering. Words are at the heart of affirmations and scripts, two powerful tools that will help you take control of your thinking. When you take the time to consciously write out what you would like to see, feel, or hear at any given time with strong, empowering language, and then read that back to yourself, those ideas sink into your subconscious, changing how you act over time.

▲ Use Imagination

Visualization, long practiced in the world of sport, is another great tool to create the results you are seeking. Essentially, you imagine the experience and/or positive outcome that you want to happen in as much detail as possible. This might conjure up a picture in your mind, or a feeling in your body, or tap into your other senses in some way. Remember, what you see is what you get. Pay attention to what images you have in your mind, especially at the subconscious level, as they are likely to come true.

This trait comes down to a really simple idea. Control your thoughts or let them control you. If you are not getting the results you are looking for, check in with what you are thinking!

DEBBIE: I was sitting by myself in the bleachers staring at the blue water of the empty Olympic-size pool and letting my imagination roam. As I watched, the pool came alive. I saw us on the deck getting ready for the finals at the Olympics. I was talking to the swimmers just prior to them getting in and warming up. We looked relaxed and happy. We were confident. The competition approached. The judges were in place, and the announcer said, "And now representing Canada...." There was a buzz.

The entire stadium fell silent. The athletes took their positions and the music began. They dove into the water and did a 50-second underwater sequence of unimaginable difficulty. As they surfaced, the crowd roared. There was electricity in the air. I felt relieved watching as perfection unfolded in front of me.

ACHIEVERS

As the swimmers finished, the audience was on its feet. The noise was deafening. In my heart, I knew that we were the best. The marks flashed. The crowd roared. I heard the music for the medal ceremony. "Ladies and gentlemen, the Olympic champions from Canada...." I watched proudly as the flag was raised and the national anthem was played. We had won the Olympics! I had played this scene in my mind thousands of times. Eight years later my visualization of perfection came true. My thoughts became reality. We won the gold!

▲ TRAIT 7 REVIEW: Utilize Power of Thought

Utilize Power
of Thought

▲ TRAIT 7

TO BE A CHAMPION:
1. Know What Is Running Through Your Head
2. Understand How Your Thoughts Shape Your Beliefs
3. Use Your Thoughts to Drive Your Actions

ACHIEVERS

KEY CONCEPT

By mastering your thoughts, you have a much greater chance of accessing your full potential.

REALITY CHECK!

Sometimes you are not getting the results you are looking for because your thinking gets in the way. This is not as simple as thinking positive thoughts and everything will be okay, although there is some truth to it. This trait is about becoming the architect of your thinking. Increase your chances of success by paying attention to the thoughts that are running through your head.

Bring This Trait to Life

We want you to pay attention and be proactive about the words you use for the next week. Think about where you find yourself in life at the moment. What are some positive, compelling, exciting words that would be useful to think about to maximize your thoughts and actions? List 10 words that, repeated over and over, would help you see and feel how you want to be.

Generate
Enthusiasm

▲ TRAIT 8

TRAIT 8:

Generate Enthusiasm

KEY CONCEPT

Since you rarely achieve anything alone, by sharing
your passion and excitement you invite others to be
a part of the journey.

MARK: *As we wrap up the Achiever Traits, I have a confession to make. While you might imagine a top male athlete to be serious and intimidating, at heart I was also a big goof. Everyone on my swimming team always knew they could count on me to lighten things up, insert some energy, and produce a good laugh when we needed it. As I moved through my athletic career, I knew that this was an asset. In the months leading up to the Olympics, I learned how to capitalize on this by bringing more energy to what I was doing through my positive attitude.*

DEBBIE: When your ultimate objective is based around a specific moment in time, an enormous amount of pressure can accompany that. It is not uncommon to feel terrified as the big day approaches. But you can turn this around, especially by looking for ways to generate enthusiasm. For example, we knew that Mark's race was going to be on a Thursday. Around three months before the Olympics, we decided to make Thursdays a special day—the day of the week that he would really look forward to. We made it like a performance day, meaning that there was some pressure built into the training, and at the same time, we rewarded the effort with fun. We would go for dinner, coffee, a movie, whatever. At first, Mark was exhausted from his long day of training and dreaded having to do something "fun." Over time, though, when Mark woke up on each Thursday, he began to feel that something challenging but good and fun was going to happen to him.

MARK: *I had never considered that you could consciously create fun at work, but that was exactly what we did in that Olympic year. And it spread well beyond the pool. Many amateur athletes have a real challenge supporting themselves financially, and I was no exception. Following my first Olympics, I started speaking to school kids to share some of my experiences. Because I was not a bad storyteller—hyper and goofy came in handy!—I was a hit with the kids. Word spread and eventually led to my speaking to business groups, which ultimately led to appearance fees that helped support my athletic career financially. What I hadn't anticipated was the kind of energy that would come back to me from all of these people with whom I had shared my excitement. In the months leading up to my second Games, I received letters of support from thousands of people who felt a part of my journey. It was an incredible feeling to know that I had all of these people rooting for me. My positive outlook and attitude had made an impression on them, and that came back to me in a way that I could never have anticipated.*

TO BE A CHAMPION:
1. Understand That Your Attitude Sets the Tone
2. Create a Positive Ripple Effect
3. Build a Support Team

1. Understand That Your Attitude Sets the Tone

Most of the Achiever Traits have focused on how you are thinking, acting, and being. It has been all about YOU. The reality is that you rarely achieve anything in isolation. The environment you create with your attitude and outlook will be what draws other people to support you. Essentially, your attitude sets the tone for others to follow suit. When you are excited about what you are doing, other people tend to get excited, too, and will do what they can to be a part of it. Energy begets energy. Momentum builds and more gets done. And from that, success is more likely to follow.

MARK: *In my university days, I led a 'Dino' cheer for my teammates, as the dinosaur was the mascot of the University of Calgary. It consisted of rhyming words and then at the end, all of us let out a huge roar. It never failed to crack us up, and helped release some of our nervous energy. When I first joined the National team, I did the same cheer but with a different animal that represented Canada; hence, the Beaver Cheer was born. Over time, this cheer became legendary, so much so that I continue to share it with Canada's Olympic teams. As silly as it is, the energy created is totally infectious.*

2. Create a Positive Ripple Effect

The energy that you put into whatever pursuit you undertake affects the people and environment around you. Energy does beget energy, and that works both ways. It is important to know what you are sending out. The best way to get feedback is to see what kind of energy is coming back to you. Think of an Australian boomerang—whatever you throw comes back. If you are passionate, eager, absorbed, captivated, motivated, inspired, and care deeply about what you are doing, then chances are the people around you will feel the same way. They get caught up in those emotions with you. If you are detached, uninspired, disengaged, unhappy, pessimistic, and negative, then chances are you will attract others with similar dispositions. Negative or positive—what kind of ripple are you creating from the way you are behaving?

ACHIEVERS

3. Build a Support Team

When you are enthusiastic and passionate about something and you put that energy out in the world, the most incredible thing happens. You start to attract people, circumstances, and opportunities that support what you are doing. There are going to be some times when you go through really challenging circumstances. The people around you will play a major role in ensuring that you stay enthused and connected to what you are doing in those darker periods. It is important to attract good people and know that they are in your corner when you really need them. Make sure to acknowledge support, and give appreciation and thanks for the help people give. The enthusiasm and appreciation you show will come back to you many times over.

Another thing to remember when building your support team is to ask for help. Avoid letting your pride or fear stand in the way of support. There are usually many people out there who are willing to help you in some way. All you have to do is ask. If you genuinely and passionately ask for someone's help, more often than not they will give it to you. Enthusiasm, once generated, is hard to resist.

DEBBIE: Part of my current job includes acting as a mentor to coaches who are new to the Olympic scene. I find that whenever one of them phones and asks if I can help them with a particular challenge they are facing, no matter how busy I am, I cannot resist. There is something compelling that always draws me to someone who is brave enough to ask for help. Not only do I get the opportunity to share some of my knowledge and experience, I also feel more excited and enthusiastic about what they are doing because I have even more of a vested interest in their success.

▲ TRAIT 8 REVIEW: Generate Enthusiasm

TO BE A CHAMPION:

1. Understand Your Attitude Sets the Tone
2. Create a Positive Ripple Effect
3. Build a Support Team

ACHIEVERS

KEY CONCEPT

Since you rarely win anything alone, by sharing your passion and excitement you invite others to be a part of the journey.

REALITY CHECK!

We know that winning might seem like a singular pursuit. But your attitude and outlook can create excitement in many around you, supporting what you are doing in ways that you can't even imagine. Think about it. Wouldn't you rather have that collective energy of many, many people cheering you on and working for you instead of against you? It is the fun and the sharing of energy that connects you to higher levels of performance, and ultimately to your win.

Bring This Trait to Life

What are you really excited about? And whom do you share it with? All of us need a cheering squad, from close friends to work-mates. Take some time to think about what gets your energy flowing in a positive way. Now, share it with whomever you choose to be in your cheering squad. Watch to see where that energy, excitement, and enthusiasm will take you.

THE FINAL ACHIEVEMENT
Becoming a Champion

The short story before each of the eight Achiever Traits showed how these fundamental ideas guided us in the 10 months leading up to the Barcelona Olympics. All of the year's efforts had been focused toward July 30, the day of the 100-meter backstroke final. Here is what happened.

MARK: *When I woke up that morning, I knew instinctively that something good was going to happen. I could hardly wait for it to come! In the first round, there had been 65 of us competing in the preliminaries. Ultimately, 57 swimmers were eliminated, and the top 8 came back nine hours later to swim for the medals in the final. The first thing I did when I got back to the Olympic village was to call Debbie in Calgary.*

DEBBIE: It was 5 a.m. when the phone rang. Mark had qualified for the 100-meter backstroke final in second place, and I found out he was a tenth of a second behind Jeff Rouse in the qualifying rounds, with another two swimmers behind Mark by less than two-tenths of a second. We spoke for the last time before he would swim his race that night. I was as nervous and excited as he was. When we had first started this journey less than a year before, it had been Mark's absolute commitment and enthusiasm that I couldn't resist. I knew what was at stake for Mark, and how much time and energy had gone into this. It was very nerve-racking.

I knew how stressful those last 24 hours are before the race, so I had arranged a little surprise for Mark. Weeks earlier, I sat down and wrote him a letter that was only to be opened the night before the race. In it, I showed him how much I believed in him, and did it in a way that I knew would make him laugh—and remind him that he could do this.

MARK: *I was carrying that letter with me all day. For most of the time before the final, I just rested back in my room in the Olympic village. Many thoughts went through my mind, but one question I asked myself really got me thinking. "Someone has to win this race tonight. Why not me?" I jolted upright in my bed. Why not me? In the past, I would have focused on all of the things that I didn't do. This would be the time that I would defeat myself, concentrating only on what I hadn't done, letting my own insecurities take over. But this year had been so different.*

Debbie and I had worked together to make the plan that outlined all of the different things I needed to do to get here. I had made it through the brutal training sessions and had all the strength, endurance, and mental preparation I would need in the race that night.

I asked myself again, "Why not me?" I thought of coming to Barcelona early, of preparing for the crowds that night, of the mental skills workbook that had gotten me through some low points in the final weeks of preparation. I thought of the thousands of people who were cheering for me around the world. One last time, I asked myself, "Why not me?" No answer came. So I repeated the words back to myself very slowly. "Why – not – me!" I went back to the pool that night and swam the 100-meter backstroke final. When I looked to the scoreboard for the results, I don't remember seeing the time or the placing. The only thing I saw was that on the big Olympic screen, with all of the eight finalists' names, it was mine—Mark Tewksbury—that popped up first.

Eventually, I saw the time—53.98! We'd found the 1.2 seconds we'd been looking for. My dream had come true. I had the performance of my life in the moment it most mattered. I won the race in Olympic record time, and won my country's first gold medal of the Games. One of the highlights of what followed included the victory march around the pool. I had been around a long time, but never connected to the win at an Olympics or World Championship when it mattered the most. As I came to the part of the stadium where the other swimmers were sitting, one by one the teams from different countries of the world, my peers, rose and cheered, "Bravo, Mark!" I had to hold back the tears. Debbie and I had imagined an impossible win. We had done it!

KEY CONCEPT SYNOPSIS
THE ACHIEVER TRAITS
Fundamentals for Being a Champion

 By becoming a master of the question, you stay connected to yourself and to what you want to achieve.

 On the way to achieving your desired win, you must be willing to persist through tough times and periods of hard work.

 By looking at circumstances differently, you access new realms of possibility for yourself.

 By challenging yourself to tap into new ideas, you find unique solutions to move forward.

 By laying the foundation for focused action, you create a clear path to take you to your desired win.

 By mastering your thoughts, you have a much greater chance of accessing your full potential.

 By aligning your day-to-day actions with your objectives, you ensure that what you are doing will keep you on track.

 Since we rarely achieve anything alone, by sharing your passion and excitement you invite others to be a part of the journey.

ACHIEVER TRAITS—SELF-ASSESSMENT

Before moving on in this book, take the time to complete this quick, simple evaluation tool. See which Achiever Traits you need to become better at. Invest some time in them.

Rate yourself on a scale of 1 to 4:

1 = Strongly Disagree, 2 = Disagree, 3 = Agree, 4 = Strongly Agree

Achiever Trait	Personal Life	Professional Life
1. Ask Yourself Questions I am not afraid to ask myself the hard questions around what I am doing and whether it is meaningful to me.	1 2 3 4	1 2 3 4
Actions to Improve		
I take time to listen honestly to my answers and act on them.	1 2 3 4	1 2 3 4
Actions to Improve		
2. Expand Your Perspective I purposefully consider how I might have "selective awareness" in any given situation.	1 2 3 4	1 2 3 4
Actions to Improve		
I consider new ways of looking at a situation so I don't limit my access to potential solutions.	1 2 3 4	1 2 3 4
Actions to Improve		

ACHIEVERS

Achiever Trait	Personal Life	Professional Life
3. Make a Plan I am clear on what I want to achieve, identifying my win.	1 2 3 4	1 2 3 4
Actions to Improve		
I have a step-by-step plan for how I will get there.	1 2 3 4	1 2 3 4
Actions to Improve		
4. Act Effectively I evaluate my actions regularly in terms of how it relates to reaching my win.	1 2 3 4	1 2 3 4
Actions to Improve		
I make changes and revisions when necessary to allow me to be more effective.	1 2 3 4	1 2 3 4
Actions to Improve		

Achiever Trait	Personal Life	Professional Life
5. Go the Distance When faced with a setback or a very difficult task, I don't give up easily.	1 2 3 4	1 2 3 4
Actions to Improve		
I like to pay attention to the details, leaving no stone unturned.	1 2 3 4	1 2 3 4
Actions to Improve		
6. Be Innovative I am open to new, different, and better ways of doing things.	1 2 3 4	1 2 3 4
Actions to Improve		
I will take a risk and get out of my comfort zone if I think it could lead to a better way of doing something.	1 2 3 4	1 2 3 4
Actions to Improve		

ACHIEVERS

Achiever Trait		Personal Life	Professional Life
7. Utilize Power of Thought I consciously spend time considering what thoughts are going through my head and whether they are limiting or empowering.		1 2 3 4	1 2 3 4
Actions to Improve			
I purposefully use my thinking/thoughts to move me closer to my win(s).		1 2 3 4	1 2 3 4
Actions to Improve			
8. Generate Enthusiasm My attitude creates a place where people like to be around me and support me in my endeavors.		1 2 3 4	1 2 3 4
Actions to Improve			
I am able to feed off the energy and enthusiasm of those around me.		1 2 3 4	1 2 3 4
Actions to Improve			

ACHIEVERS

The Leader Traits

*Creating Champion
Organizations and Teams*

Each of the Leader Traits has a graphic icon highlighted in blue to help support the key ideas found within.

Be Aware

TRAIT 1

TRAIT ONE:
The bold blue plus sign (+) represents the heightened state of awareness that leaders need.

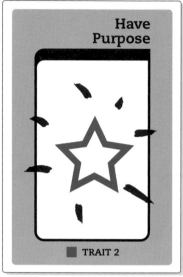

Have Purpose

TRAIT 2

TRAIT TWO:
The large blue star represents a collective purpose to be held out for others.

Create Synergy

TRAIT 3

TRAIT THREE:
The figures represent the team of people that success requires.

Show Conviction

TRAIT 4

TRAIT FOUR:
The blue heart represents the passion needed to lead others to overcome obstacles.

Use all eight icons as visual reminders of the key concepts and ideas within each of the Leader Traits.

TRAIT FIVE:
The walking C with the "e's" reminds us of the constant need for "e"ffective communication.

TRAIT SIX:
The bold first figure shows us the example we set for others.

TRAIT SEVEN:
The opposite expressions represent the contradictions we all face.

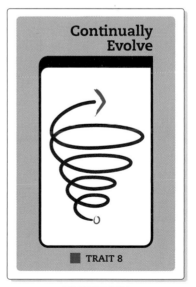

TRAIT EIGHT:
The upward spiral represents the need to constantly grow.

In the Leader Traits, we take you on the next step of your *Great Traits* **Champion's Journey**. This section outlines a set of eight leadership fundamentals that provide a rock-solid foundation for great things to happen for yourself *and* for those you lead.

Being a champion from a leadership perspective means you create winning results for the organizations and teams you lead, you ensure each person brings out his or her strengths, and you make sure many different people can contribute their personal best to the overall success of an organization. These traits create the environment needed for you and those you lead to succeed.

You may have noticed the triangle imagery in the Achiever section. It is a reference to striving for the pinnacle—your best—that underlines the idea of achievement. In the Leader Traits, you will see the shape of a square. This is a play on the idea that as a leader, you are back at square one and need to provide the foundational base for others to succeed. The square represents the solid foundation you create that enables others to reach for their best.

Leadership requires a different set of skills than achievement, although many of the ideas that were introduced in the Achiever Traits are built upon in this section. Just because you were a super achiever doesn't mean you are automatically a great leader. Enabling others to become champions is something entirely different, and is what this next section explores.

Each Leader Trait begins with a story from us. We then identify a key concept that describes what we mean for that particular trait. Following that, we have learning objectives and anecdotes that bring the trait to life. At the end, there is a Review section with a summary and questions to help you master that particular Leader Trait.

Many of us are leaders whether we realize it or not. CEOs are obviously leaders, but so are coaches, parents, community activists, teachers, and many others who take on the roles and the responsibility of creating a winning environment for others day in and day out.

By mastering the Leader Traits, you not only create the environment necessary for others to achieve great things, you also build the foundation to master the final set of Great Traits coming next in Legacy.

The second step in your *Champion's Journey* starts here and now. Enjoy!

Be Aware

TRAIT 1

TRAIT 1:
Be Aware

KEY CONCEPT
The greater your awareness, the greater your capacity
to act effectively as a leader.

DEBBIE: I clearly remember early in my career, over 30 years ago, when I led my team to a breakthrough success for the first time. We had won every event at the national championships. It was an amazing feat. Everyone kept commenting on how well positioned we were for a repeat performance at next year's world championship trials. We were a shoe-in. That was exactly when my fear and doubt set in.

On the surface, everything seemed fine. I'd faithfully show up at work every day, well prepared. But inside I was consumed with negative thinking and self-doubt. For the entire year, I kept asking myself, "How could we possibly repeat that success?" Suddenly, the stakes seemed so much higher, the pressure enormous. I worried about how embarrassed and humiliated I'd be when we failed to repeat our success. I thought about how badly I'd feel for the athletes when they didn't do as well as expected.

Did we lose? You bet we did!

I never made the connection between my thinking and my coaching performance. Initially, I blamed the judges. The beauty of being in a subjective sport is that you can always blame it on the judges! But in the end, I had to face the truth: Most of the blame lay with me. My negative thoughts were a major reason we had lost. So why didn't I just change my thinking? I couldn't. I wasn't even conscious of what was going on in my head until it was all over.

Had I been more aware during that fateful year, I could have found ways to reframe the fear and worry, to change my thinking to be more empowering. That, in turn, would have improved my ability to connect the athletes to their full potential. Instead, I found myself getting angry easily during training, taking out my fear of failing on the athletes. I would berate *them* for making mistakes. I constantly focused on how bad things looked and how we would never win if we were swimming like this. Everything the athletes did just reinforced my mindset that we were going to lose.

My behavior had a profound impact on the day-to-day performance of the swimmers. More than ever before, they were continually calling in sick. And that only made my fear and panic worse. In turn, that weakened the athletes' performances. It became a self-fulfilling prophecy. Because of my lack of awareness, I could see very few possibilities for making the situation better. In my mind, I couldn't see us winning. I was overwhelmed with fear, which limited my approach the entire year. Negative thinking led to bad decisions and subsequent actions, which led to disappointing results. It was a very tough lesson to learn.

TO BE A GREAT LEADER:
1. Awareness Starts With You
2. Pay Attention to Others
3. Influence What Is Happening Around You

1. Awareness Starts With You

We begin this trait with increasing your internal awareness, becoming more cognizant of what you are thinking, and consciously making the connection that your thoughts drive your actions and behavior. This takes us back to Achiever Trait 7: Utilize Power of Thought. As you begin the leadership traits, remember that being aware always starts with you. The first step as a leader is to check in with yourself to make sure your own thinking is where you want it to be.

A mistake many leaders make is that they let their own issues of doubt and fear get in the way of leading others. They project or take things personally and often don't even realize they are doing it. By heightening your internal awareness, you can make changes before it is too late. You can consciously decide what to think or what actions to take to be much more effective. A simple way to tap into this is to ask some key questions:

- What am I thinking in this situation?
- Is there any doubt or negativity attached to my thinking?
- How can I make sure I do not limit myself and/or others with this way of thinking?

The great news here is that awareness is curative. Becoming aware of what needs to be changed is often enough to make the shift. At the very least, once something is brought to the surface of your consciousness, you can do something about it.

2. Pay Attention to Others

Heightened awareness as a leader is hugely important for two reasons. First, your thinking not only impacts you, but also those you lead. As shown in the Awareness Cycle on the next page, what is going on in your head directly impacts others' ability to tap into their own potential, which determines their actions and impacts their results. As a leader, your thoughts, actions, and behavior influence the ability of the people you lead to access *their* full potential.

LEADERS

The Awareness Cycle

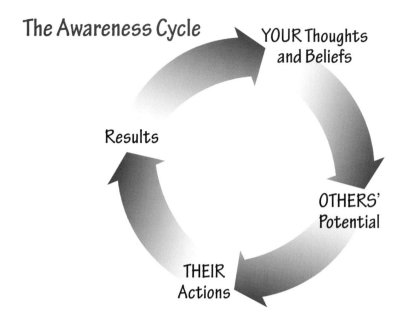

YOUR Thoughts and Beliefs

OTHERS' Potential

THEIR Actions

Results

Secondly, your heightened awareness as a leader enables you to help others become aware of their own thinking—their thought cycles. It is your job as the leader to find the most effective way to positively impact others' thoughts to help them access their own potential.

How are *their* thoughts and actions impacting *their* performance? Great leaders can have a major impact on those they are leading simply by helping them become more aware of themselves.

MARK: *Many years ago, I was at a practice in the middle of a heavy training period and was poisoning the team with my negativity. I was being sarcastic, pulling a face as each instruction was given to us, bad-mouthing the coach behind his back. I was completely unaware of how I was single-handedly bringing down the entire group until the coach pulled me aside and pointed out what a negative impact I was having. He asked me what was going on, and helped me become aware of what I was thinking and feeling, and how that was translating into my actions. I knew from then on that whenever I was feeling down, I had to be much more aware of how my negativity was sabotaging the team. My coach, by making me more self-aware, helped me access more of my potential.*

Trait 1: Be Aware ■ 79

Notice what is happening with the people you are leading. Find the "coachable moments." When things are working, make sure you tell them so they become more aware and continue to do even better. The same is true when things aren't working, so they can change. Your ability to find "coachable moments" is directly connected to your capacity to be aware of yourself and others.

3. Influence What Is Happening Around You

The final part of this trait is paying attention to what is happening around you in your external environment. Be aware of how larger events might have an impact on your reality. We do not live or work in silos. Notice what you notice, understanding that outside forces can potentially impact your outcome. The more you see of what is going on, the greater your chance of influencing the environment around you to get you where you want to go.

DEBBIE: In the four years leading up to the Sydney Olympics, I worked with the Australian synchronized swimming team. They were ranked last in the world, and I had the challenge of getting them to place in the top eight. Each year, our routines and technical skill improved dramatically, but each year we would come back with the same result, the bottom of the pack. Even though we became much better than other countries, we just couldn't move ahead. I couldn't figure out what was wrong. It was very frustrating.

Eventually, in one of those "ah-ha!" moments, it came to me. I blamed the judges again, but this time with reason. It was the judges' selective awareness that was not allowing them to see how good we were really getting. In order to justify placing us at the bottom, where they were used to seeing us, the judges were only noticing the things we were doing wrong and not what we were doing right. When these same judges marked the top teams, they took the opposite approach, noticing only what they liked so they could justify putting them in the top half of the field. Coming from a country that was always in the medals, I had never been aware of this phenomenon, and why would I as long as we were winning. How could I lead these judges to look at us in a different light?

At the next competition, I asked a couple of judges what they noticed that the Australians were doing right. As expected, they had no answers.

LEADERS

But the question shifted their awareness so that the next time they judged us, they started to look at what was working, largely because they knew I would come and ask them. This was the turning point for us. They started to notice what we were doing well and our marks went up accordingly. Eventually, we made it into the finals at the World Championships and top eight at the Olympics, a first for Australia in front of their hometown crowd at the 2000 Sydney Games.

■ TRAIT 1 REVIEW: Be Aware

TO BE A GREAT LEADER:

1. Awareness Starts With You
2. Pay Attention to Others
3. Influence What Is Happening Around You

KEY CONCEPT

The greater your awareness, the greater your capacity to act effectively as a leader.

REALITY CHECK!

As leaders, it is easy to fall into a state of unawareness as we go through our day-to-day routine. If you are projecting your own doubts onto those you are leading, you hold them back. You need to know what is going on with yourself and with those you are leading, as well as look for ways to influence the environment around you. By keeping your awareness levels high, you can better connect those around you to their full potential.

Bring This Trait to Life

As different situations unfold, check in with yourself:

- Are you aware of your own thoughts, actions, and their impact?
- Are you paying attention to the thoughts and actions of others?
- Are you finding ways to influence your external environment for the better?

LEADERS

TRAIT 2:

Have Purpose

KEY CONCEPT

By capturing people's imagination with clear objectives and roles, you inspire everyone to do their part in making it happen.

DEBBIE: In the world of sport, Canada was notorious for one embarrassing distinction. It was the only country in Olympic history to host the Olympic Games and not win a gold medal on home soil. And it happened not just once, but twice—in the summer of 1976 and the winter of 1988.

When Vancouver was awarded the 2010 Winter Olympics, Mark Lowry, the Director of Sport for the Canadian Olympic Committee, saw that something drastic had to change within the sport system or Canada would run the risk of repeating its lack of gold on home soil.

Historically, funding for athletes within the sport system was extremely fragmented. Many different bodies (funding partners), from Sport Canada to corporate Canada to the Canadian Olympic Committee to universities (and there are more), all gave support money, but none of this was coordinated. The various partners in the sport system also took the approach of giving everyone a little as opposed to looking where our biggest return on investment could be. Mark knew that just because Canada had won the right to host the 2010 Games, it did not mean more money for everyone. He saw that if he could get all of the various funding partners on side, then Canada could best maximize the money that *was* in the system already.

Mark held out a vision that challenged people to reconsider how things were done. He shared his idea of what could happen, and expressed the need to target the funds where they could make the most difference. It was controversial and somehow "unCanadian" to focus resources solely on those sports with potential to win medals, while cutting other non-performing sports completely out of the funding. The process wasn't easy at first, but Mark knew it was the only way to proceed if Canada wanted to win medals, specifically gold medals, in Vancouver.

He began with his own organization, the Canadian Olympic Committee. All monies that were available to athletes within his reach went into a targeted high-performance fund. The Canadian Sport Review Panel was born, a committee of technical experts assigned to review all of the Olympic sports. This committee's task was to determine which sports would have the most medal potential if they were to receive additional financial resources to run world-class programs for their athletes. I was honoured to be a part of this inaugural committee, interviewing and evaluating sports, and ultimately determining the best way to spend the limited resources we had. It was from here that Own the Podium emerged, an organization whose mission is to lead the development of Canadian sports to achieve sustainable performances at the Olympic and Paralympic Games.

Results started to show with several of our targeted athletes winning medals at the Athens Olympics in 2004. The funding partners also wanted to be a part of this more focused approach. Mark's philosophy of providing every Canadian athlete who had medal potential with the resources they would need to be able to compete against the best in the world and win took hold.

Sadly, Mark Lowry died of cancer in 2005, but his vision continued to come to life. In Torino, 2006, Canada had its best results ever. In 2008, we had our best Summer Olympic results since 1996. Different leadership took over the program, but the vision never faltered from that which Mark held out. Canada not only won gold on home soil in 2010, it won 14 gold medals! This was a new record for the total number of gold medals won by any country at a Winter Olympics.

LEADERS

TO BE A GREAT LEADER:
1. Set a Compelling Vision
2. Bring the Vision to Life
3. Keep Everyone on Track

1. Set a Compelling Vision

A great vision is compelling, awesome, and filled with possibility. It answers the question: What are we here to do? It acts as the driving force—the purpose—that every organization needs in order to be successful.

The first step of this trait is to identify an inspiring vision for the future. This provides a clear overriding objective for the organization, and every person who is a part of it, to achieve. We cannot emphasize how important this is. Setting a compelling vision means people see the larger purpose, and then they can picture their own part in making it happen. When done right, people take responsibility and commit because they see their work is meaningful.

MARK: *A few years ago, I was asked to moderate a conference that brought together the leaders of patient advocacy groups from across Canada. These were the people who were on the front line of their organizations, pushing to get more support and government funding for their individual causes. Traditionally, these leaders had worked against each other, each trying to show why their particular disease or patient's situation was more important than the others in order to secure the most money possible. Cancer was more urgent than mental health, which was more important than diabetes, which was more pressing than heart and stroke, which should take greater priority than AIDS. And on it went. As we moved through the agenda, tensions continued to grow, and no progress was being made. We kept finding ourselves back at square one as one group or another hijacked the program, claiming that their needs should take priority over the others.*

LEADERS

At one point in the meeting, a question was asked. "Can we all agree that our patients, regardless of the disease, deserve access to the best care imaginable?" Everyone could get behind that. "Working from that premise, what if we all put our individual energy together to lobby for the greater good of patients in the country?" With that simple question, a new and different vision came over the group. They left the meeting willing to work together for the first time, each with the patient at the centre of their vision. And collectively, they accessed much more funding than had ever been possible before.

2. Bring the Vision to Life

Once everyone is clear on what the overarching vision is, the next step is to engage each person (including yourself) in understanding their **SPECIFIC** role in bringing that vision to life, and the goals they need to set to make it happen. You need to get people excited about what they are doing. Make sure each person knows how he or she directly contributes. Does everyone in the organization understand how their individual roles and goals align with the overall success of the organization?

Following the **SHOT** formula (Specifically, Honestly, Outline, Time-line), the next step is to **HONESTLY** assess where you and your team are in relation to achieving its part of the overall organizational objective. This is the distinction of planning as a leader as opposed to an achiever; you are now called upon to be *in consultation with others* to ensure all individual contributions lead to realizing the vision.

This is your chance to take score with your team and to assess where you really are. This can be tough, especially for you as the leader. Facing the facts isn't always easy, but don't sugarcoat things. It is much better to be brutally honest up front than to miss your objectives in the future because you weren't willing to acknowledge where you really were. Planning is the "how" to bring the vision to life. In order to make the best coordinated plan for you and your team, you need to find the right starting point.

MARK: *I spoke recently to an organization that had an ambitious vision: to deliver the most spectacular travel experience in the world. Great. But within that vision, the leaders' challenge was to have the thousand-plus* *employees plan how they were going to bring that idea to life for themselves. They did that by having each person consider how they would fill in the following blank: "I am going to bring spectacular to life by _____." People took it and ran with it, carrying a card on them at work that reminded them everyday of what their personal objective was. "I will provide spectacular service, or spectacular greetings, or spectacular safety." This simple exercise made it clear to each individual how his or her role contributed to bringing the larger organizational purpose to life. And it solidified this company's position as one of the best high-end travel providers in the world.*

3. Keep Everyone on Track

Now that you know where you are in relation to where you want to go, the next step is to look at how you are going to close the gap. Make an **OVERVIEW** of the collective actions that have to be taken and the numerous benchmarks that need to be attained in order to reach the ultimate objective. As you and your team are determining what actions need to be taken, always keep in mind that overarching organizational objective. By aligning everyone's daily actions and benchmarks with where the organization ultimately wants to go, you ensure that what you are doing will keep you on track. How will you and those you are leading know success is being achieved on a daily basis?

Great leaders make sure people are not just busy doing things, but are busy doing the *right* things. With many people doing many different tasks, it is also hugely important that you are coordinating your action plans with other departments and groups to ensure you are not in conflict with each other or duplicating work. Alignment at every level is crucial to success.

The final step in the planning process is to attach **TIMELINES** to the various actions and benchmarks that have been identified. These become the measuring stick by which you, the leader, can assess whether things are working or not. Your job is not just to have the best plan; it is also to be able to execute that plan in the best way possible. Evaluation is the key to this.

The ability to meet your timelines and your benchmarks becomes your key performance indicator. This helps determine if you are on track or if you need to change what you and your team are doing. If you or someone you are leading misses a timeline or a benchmark, you need to determine why. Make sure you are measuring the right thing. Did you establish the right timeline? Was an inappropriate benchmark set? Were the actions taken actually effective? Upon your evaluation, make appropriate revisions.

Evaluation gives people feedback to make sure they are executing effectively, and doing their individual part in a meaningful way that brings the overall vision to life.

■ TRAIT 2 REVIEW: Have Purpose

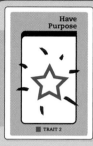

TO BE A GREAT LEADER:
1. Set a Compelling Vision
2. Bring the Vision to Life
3. Keep Everyone on Track

KEY CONCEPT
By capturing people's imagination with clear objectives and roles, you inspire everyone to do their part in making it happen.

REALITY CHECK!
It is ironic that what we often stray furthest from as leaders is our purpose. Many of us simply get caught in reactionary mode. As distraction after distraction come hurling toward you, you might forget to see how your decisions actually connect back to that original raison d'être. You had a purpose, but if you have strayed from it and aren't acting effectively, then what are you doing? Really keeping the purpose in mind gives clarity and guides decision making, keeping you and those you lead on track.

Bring This Trait to Life
As different situations unfold, check in with yourself:

- Have you set a compelling vision?
- Are people clear on their role in achieving that vision?
- Have you established clear targets and benchmarks to measure progress along the way?

LEADERS

TRAIT 3:
Create Synergy

KEY CONCEPT
By bringing together the right people, an inexplicable energy is created that produces outstanding results much greater than any one individual's contribution.

DEBBIE: After the Los Angeles Olympics, I wasn't satisfied with winning two silver medals. It was hard to settle for second when I knew we had the potential to win. In reflecting back, I realized that one of the reasons we hadn't won gold was because I had wanted to do it all by myself. I thought I didn't need any help. Unfortunately, I had been driven from a place of ego, and I didn't want to share the journey or the glory with anyone else. Thankfully, I realized that if we were going to be successful at the next Olympics, I couldn't do it all alone. To be the best, I needed to build a support team of experts around me.

One of the goals was to be physically better than we had ever been before, doing things with a higher degree of difficulty than anyone in the world had seen. The challenge was that I didn't know how to train for this. I had heard about Dr. David Smith, jokingly known as Doctor Death by the athletes, an exercise physiologist renowned for his intense and difficult testing programs. In Dr. Smith, I found the right person to take care of the first objective.

A fundamental part of our success would be determined by how we were judged. Although how we were marked was ultimately out of my control, I wanted to do what I could to make the international judges a part of the process. Working with Synchro Canada, our national organization, we held a seminar where we showcased our Olympic athletes to get the judges' input on what they liked and what suggestions they might have for improving the routine. This was a bit unconventional, and strange as it may sound, these judges became a part of our support team.

One of the greatest lessons from my first Olympics was how important the homefield advantage had been for the Americans at the 1984 Los Angeles Games. As the next Games were to be held in Seoul, I wanted to find ways to connect with a Korean audience as though we were the hometown favorites. A Korean/Canadian woman, Mrs. Chang, filled this role perfectly. She had been an interpreter for a visiting Korean national team at the Pan Pacific Championships earlier that year in Calgary. She took us to Korea in March of the Olympic year and, because she was connected to so many important people in Korea, was invaluable to us. We did water shows, gave clinics with the up-and-coming Korean national team athletes, visited schools, and received media attention. The Koreans, although not a medal threat, were working to build their program, and we could help them. It was a great exchange. All of these actions built relationships so that when we came back to the Olympics, the Koreans remembered and supported us.

The two gold medals we won would have never been possible without the support and expertise of the people I asked to work with us. Each person was clear on their role and what they needed to do. Everyone, from Dr. Smith to the judges, to Mrs. Chang and beyond, took pride in making the overall objective of winning the Olympics a reality.

TO BE A GREAT LEADER:

1. Get the Right People in the Right Roles
2. Guide Your Team to High Performance
3. Keep the Team Performing at Its Best

1. Get the Right People in the Right Roles

When building a team, the greater your clarity of purpose, the better able you are to identify the right people required to be successful. This trait builds on Trait 2: Have Purpose, because once you have a clear organizational outcome, you know what you have to rally your team around.

With your purpose in place, you can then determine what kind of people you need to have on your team from two important fundamental perspectives: skill base and personality. The skill-based side is pretty obvious; you have been trained to do something and have experience in a certain area. The organization requires a specific function, and you match it. On the other side, you bring your unique indelible personality stamp to the team. We call this your "X" factor. It is this combination of skill and personality that often creates the magic that makes teams work.

By virtue of filling the specific roles with the right people required to meet your team's needs, you will bring the right collection of individuals together. When people are able to maximize their skills *and* their personality *and* work well with others on the team, you will know you have it. The likelihood of reaching your objectives increases substantially with this kind of synergy.

2. Guide Your Team to High Performance

Synergy is the outcome of a carefully guided process. As a leader, you have to understand the dynamic phases through which teams form. A couple of skills are needed to do this. First, you need to call upon the awareness developed in Trait One: Be Aware in order to identify where your team is. Then, if they are not at the high-performing level, you need to be able to move them there. From our experience (and adapted from team-building theory), we have identified and given a brief description of the five dynamic phases involved in building teams.

The Five Dynamic Phases of Team

- **Dynamic Phase 1: Meet and Greet**
  You come together as a team and meet each other. Everyone is on guard, polite but cautious. If the team is doing well, it is because people are doing their individual parts effectively. It will take some time to become consistently effective as a team.

LEADERS

■ **Dynamic Phase 2: True Colors**
The team gets to know each other. Relationships begin to form. Cliques and alliances emerge. Some confrontation and arguments might unfold. Generally, the team members are not committed to the collective purpose or to each other yet, remaining focused on themselves and their own individual tasks.

■ **Dynamic Phase 3: Clicking Together**
A process is formed around how to work together. The group begins making decisions and finding solutions. People feel committed to the collective objective and are willing to evaluate their own effectiveness.

■ **Dynamic Phase 4: High Performance**
The team is firing on all cylinders, completing work efficiently, effectively, and seemingly effortlessly. People feel confident and supported, and are open to each other's ideas. Roles are clear, and real progress is made. There is excitement to push the bar higher with everyone feeding off the collective momentum of the group. There is an underlying resourcefulness, flexibility, and joy in working together.

■ **Dynamic Phase 5: Declining Performance**
The team is self-satisfied, complacent, and bored. Self-interest is evident; ideas are no longer challenged as patterns set in. Criticism is seen as disloyalty and may be followed by isolation or rejection. The team enters into a period of decline.

As the leader, once you've identified where your team is, then you can create some specific strategies to get everyone to the high-performing phase.

MARK: *Following my athletic career, I joined the International Olympic Committee as part of the site selection commission. Basically, 15 of us from different parts of the world and varying backgrounds came together to create a team whose purpose was to evaluate the bids from the 11 cities vying to host the 2004 Olympics. Each member was chosen for his or her particular expertise—myself as the athlete, someone else for security, another for the environment, and so on. It was a very challenging experience because our mission had to be completed in just three months, so we had to gel as a team very quickly.*

At our first stop, each of us performed well in our own area of exper-tise, but we worked in isolation from each other. In the second city, two of our members were at each other's throats. By the third city, we had over-come the initial hostility and awkwardness, gotten to know each other, and had found the best ways to work together. By the fourth city, we had hit our stride, effortlessly and quickly evaluating whether a city was right to host the Games or not. It didn't take long for the team to come together, largely because we were all allowed to do what we did best.

The challenge was that we became so good at working together as a team that we soon became complacent. After staying in the high-performance mode for four or five cities, we started to lose focus, began fighting with each other, and individuals started to feel ostracized. The head of the commission wasn't aware of the team dynamics because his political interests prevailed over the needs of the team. By the time we arrived in our final cities, we were a team in decline, interfering with each other's respective roles, and no longer honoring the high-functioning group we had once been.

3. Keep the Team Performing at Its Best

Synergy doesn't just happen. You have to create the environment for it. In order to get to the high-performing phase, there are six essential elements required. They work together and lay the foundation for real synergy and outstanding results to happen.

1. **Clear Vision of the Desired Outcome**
   - ❏ Everyone has a clear picture of what he or she is working toward.
   - ❏ The vision acts as the guiding force and has a sense of awe and possibility all at the same time.
   - ❏ Everyone shares the vision and is willing to do his or her part to bring it to life.

2. **Clear Roles**
   - ❏ Every individual in the organization has a clear primary role to play that will ultimately impact the overall success of the team.
   - ❏ Each individual is clear on what his or her role is, as well as every-one else's.

- ❏ On a less obvious level, everyone plays a secondary role. This role may be less easily identified as it pertains to the unique behavioral quality that each person brings (e.g., the "cheerleader").
- ❏ The secondary role allows the unique personality of an individual to come out and enhance the team.

3. **Focus of Attention**
- ❏ To do anything at a world-class level, the focus must be on the task at hand with full concentration, uninterrupted by limiting thoughts, self-doubt, external influences, or others' negative energy.
- ❏ There is a sense of being relaxed yet very focused as everything flows effortlessly.

4. **Strong Belief in Self and Group**
- ❏ Even though there may be strong differences of opinion, there is an underlying belief or trust that everyone wants the same outcome.
- ❏ While at certain times belief in self may wane, the group is there as support and to bring each other back on track when required.
- ❏ Each person strongly believes that he or she is an integral part of the team's being able to achieve its objectives.

5. **Sense of Accomplishment**
- ❏ At the end of each day or working session, there is a belief that each person is getting closer to achieving his or her objectives.
- ❏ There is never a sense of having wasted time.
- ❏ Even if it isn't going as smoothly as desired, there is still a feeling of accomplishment because there is a basic understanding that kinks need to be worked out and it won't always go perfectly.

6. **Delight in Others' Excellence**
- ❏ You appreciate when others are excellent at what they do.
- ❏ The organization finds ways to celebrate and recognize the successes of individuals and groups.
- ❏ Everyone in the organization has the opportunity to shine.

As the leader, keep focusing and building upon these six essential elements. They lay the foundation for the kind of synergy required to reach high levels of performance as a team.

DEBBIE: Because of my experience in developing Olympic and world champions, I was part of a group brought together to work with many different sports within the national system. Our purpose was to help the various organizations that we targeted create the environment necessary for their athletes to achieve high levels of performance. In this job, I was joined by several world-class experts, all of us excited to be working together toward a common goal: creating a world-class, high-performance sport culture in Canada resulting in more Olympic, Paralympic, and World Championship medals.

Although we were all clear on the vision and roles we were to play, it became evident early on that the project leader did not think that each of us actually had the expertise, knowledge, and know-how to make this happen. Instead of believing in us to do the job in the way we thought would work, he told us exactly what and how to do it. You can imagine how well this went over with a group of high performers, all of whom were proud of their abilities and used to being allowed to do what they do best. There was no room to share the enormous collective knowledge that we brought to the group. As the weeks progressed, feelings of frustration, cynicism, and uselessness set in as we were kept busier and busier doing things that, in our minds, had nothing to do with reaching the common goal. With each new "make work" project, we lost more and more enthusiasm and commitment to the job. We had no sense of accomplishment or ownership to the project because we seemed to be straying further and further from what we had been brought together to do.

As we tried to explain to him why some of the things he was making us do were not the best way to go, he simply became angry and even more dictatorial. There was no desire left to succeed and, ultimately, the team fell apart not having accomplished what it set out to do.

LEADERS

■ TRAIT 3 REVIEW: Create Synergy

TO BE A GREAT LEADER:

1. Get the Right People in the Right Roles
2. Guide Your Team to High Performance
3. Keep the Team Performing at Its Best

KEY CONCEPT

By bringing together the right people, an inexplicable energy is created that produces outstanding results much greater than any one individual's contribution.

REALITY CHECK!

Where leaders fall down is often for one of two reasons. First, they don't get the best people in the identified roles and let them do what they do best. Second, they don't create the team environment needed for high performance to happen. Pay attention to the essentials required for outstanding results. When you create synergy, you have a team of people who are individually great at what they do, and together are even greater.

Bring This Trait to Life

As different situations unfold, check in with yourself:

- Are you getting the right people in the right roles in order to fulfill a specific purpose?
- Which of the five phases of team is your team in?
- What needs to happen to get to the high-performing phase?

TRAIT 4

TRAIT 4:

Show Conviction

KEY CONCEPT

By believing completely in what you are doing, it enables
you and those you lead to achieve outstanding results.

MARK: *In 2001, I was part of a team from Montreal that won the right
to host a major international event, The Gay Games. It was to be the
largest in the movement's history, with 16,000 participants expected. Along
with sport and culture, for the first time ever in sport history, including the
Olympic Games, we were organizing an internationally recognized human rights conference that would be opened by the United Nations High
Commissioner. It would be a spectacular gathering. But then disaster
struck. After two years of negotiating, we failed to come to an agreement
with the governing body of the event. Halfway to delivering the Games,
they were stripped from us and given to another city. Needless to say, we
found ourselves in a most difficult situation.*

*In regrouping, we came to many realizations. We had a clear vision
for what this event could be. We had a solid plan to make it happen.
All of our financial partners agreed to stay with us if we decided to go
ahead with games under a different name. Even though the challenge was
enormous and there were many times when it would have been easy to*

give up, we had an undying belief in what we were doing. So, we created a new event. Personally, I was convinced that within the gay sport movement something had to change, and that we were the right group of people in the right city to make it happen. But, unless the participants came, all of this was for nothing. And in order to get them onside, we had to win their trust and confidence.

On a snowy, blizzard weekend in January, we invited sport leaders from around the world to join us in Montreal to explain what had happened when we lost the Gay Games, and to look forward toward the future. There were representatives from Australia, the United States, Canada, Germany, Denmark, and a few South American countries. The mood was challenging, with many people unclear about what had really happened in the negotiating process, and doubtful whether they should support us in Montreal. After two days of meetings, it came down to a moment when a decision would have to be made. With this group's support, we could have our Games; without it, we were finished.

I was the person who had to make that final pitch. With passion and conviction I shared our vision for the future, I explained how we had arrived at this moment, and then asked the leaders if they believed a new organization was necessary to move forward. One by one the leaders stood and said the old way wasn't working. The vote was unanimous. The Outgames were born.

TO BE A GREAT LEADER:

1. Be Passionate About What You Are Doing
2. Get Through the Tough Times
3. Strengthen Confidence in Others

1. Be Passionate About What You Are Doing

Of all the leadership traits, this one is the most difficult to articulate because it represents the essence of a leader. Conviction is the spirit you bring to leadership, and is a major factor in determining how successful you will be. Your beliefs—and commitment to them—are powerful driving forces and form your conviction. When someone is passionate about what he or she is doing, it is inspiring. You can't help but be drawn to them. You believe in what they say and do. It is why conviction is so fundamental to leaders. Would you really follow someone who didn't believe completely in what they are doing?

That is not to say that as a leader you won't have moments of self-doubt and questioning. You will. There are times when you won't know what will happen, when uncertainty and fear are real. These periods are simply tests. When they happen, great leaders take the time to self-reflect. Question yourself and what you are doing. In doing so, you will find that you have a renewed sense of passion, belief, and commitment about what you are doing—all powerful driving forces behind conviction.

DEBBIE: Following a silver medal finish in the duet event at the Los Angeles Olympics, the Canadian synchronized swimming program was determined to bring home gold four years later in Seoul. To do that, the national governing body, Synchro Canada, believed that our top two technically ranked athletes, Carolyn Waldo and Sylvie Frechette, should be partnered. In theory, this made perfect sense and seemed like a logical route for them to pursue.

I believed passionately that a different strategy would be required to succeed. Although Carolyn and Sylvie were technically the best, I knew winning would require much more than numbers adding up on paper. The duet event requires perfect synergy between two athletes—everything from body size to mental connection mattered. It was also my belief that the athletes needed to train together day in and day out for the full four years to create the best routine. From my perspective, the best match to bring home gold was to partner Carolyn with another swimmer, Michelle Cameron.

This was a hugely unpopular decision. The pressure to swim Carolyn with Sylvie was relentless, but I believed so much in my strategy that I

LEADERS

was willing to put it all on the line. Two years out from the Olympics, we paired Carolyn and Michelle together for the World Championships. Frustrated with this constant doubting and questioning from the Synchro community, I told them that if they did not win I was willing to re-examine the situation and make a change, but if they won I didn't ever want to hear another complaint. Winning gold in the duet at the world championships in Madrid was a wonderful experience for many reasons. It really brought home for me the notion of not ever giving up in something you really believe can happen. Not only did it start a winning path for Carolyn and Michelle that led to gold at the Olympics in Seoul, Sylvie would go on to become an Olympic champion herself in the solo event in Barcelona four years later.

2. Get Through the Tough Times

No matter what, there will be challenging times. It is inevitable. Belief in what you are doing, and in your ability to do it, is what gets you through. It is your unwavering conviction that enables you to overcome enormous challenges. This is the trait that gives you *and* those you lead the determination to succeed against all odds.

Your conviction as a leader significantly impacts those around you. Your belief in the purpose, along with your confidence in the ability of those you are leading enables them to also endure major setbacks. But be aware! If you don't really believe, then this has some serious implications. If you give up on yourself, you are giving up on those you are leading, too. Your conviction is absolutely fundamental to the team's overall success.

Being able to come back after failure is never easy. This skill, which is fueled by conviction, differentiates great leaders from others. Your ability to "get back to it" becomes a competitive edge over time. When others are licking their wounds, or giving up too soon, you are able to navigate through the tough times and refocus on what needs to be done.

MARK: *One of the legends of my sport was a Soviet swimmer named Vladimir Salnikov. He burst onto the international scene as a 16-year-old finalist at the 1976 Olympics in the 1500-meter freestyle, the marathon of swimming. In the years following those Olympics, Vladimir dominated his event, and was all set to win gold in front of a hometown crowd at the*

1980 Moscow Olympics four years later. Although he became an Olympic champion, the western countries had boycotted the Games, and the win seemed empty. So Vladimir kept swimming for four more years. Still at the top of the world rankings, a remarkable feat in itself, he was prepared to defend his title at the 1984 Los Angeles Olympics. Two months before the Games were to begin, the eastern bloc countries of the world boycotted, and Vladimir never got his chance to prove himself.

Vladimir decided to keep swimming following the boycott, wanting to win an Olympic gold medal when the entire world was there. In 1986, though, he didn't make the final at the World Championships. As he prepared for the 1988 Seoul Olympics, everyone gave up on him. At 28 years old, the world agreed that his dream was impossible. So what did he do? Vladimir fired all of his coaches, took the reins, and built a team around himself that he led with his undying conviction. I was there when he touched the wall first and became the oldest gold medalist in our sport's history.

3. Strengthen Confidence in Others

It is important not to confuse bravado with conviction. When the going gets really brutal, and someone's encouragement is based on bravado and groundless ideas, there is no substance to the message and everything falls apart accordingly. Bravado never takes root. Only conviction, aligned with purpose, enables things to grow.

When you have a firm resolve in yourself, in others, and in doing what needs to be done, people will respond positively. Your conviction spreads. It unlocks the potential in people, helping them achieve outstanding results. Your spirit ripples to others, giving the people you lead added confidence and strength as they strive to reach their full potential. Conviction is often that little extra that enables people to override their limiting beliefs and break them through to a higher level of performance.

DEBBIE: For several years, I have worked with national team coaches from different sports. My role was to advise them on how to improve their on-the-job performance. It was in the way that the coaches spoke about their teams that gave away their level of conviction to me. What I noticed was that whenever their teams or athletes had success, many of the coaches

LEADERS

would talk from the "we" perspective. "*We* rose to the challenge today" or "*We* put in the hard work." Whenever they had disappointing results, all of a sudden the talk became about "they." "*They* underperformed" or "*They* got complacent and lazy out there." The coaches weren't taking responsibility for the team when it wasn't doing well. Who is going to give it all for someone who in the heat of the battle turns from *we* to *they*?

From the team's point of view, the coaches believed in them only when they were succeeding. When this was brought to the coaches' attention, it allowed them to see how their conviction appeared to be wavering when times got tough. Their unwavering conviction was fundamental to success. The coaches had to find ways to show they believed in the hard times as well as the good times to ensure they were strengthening the confidence of the team and not undermining it.

■ TRAIT 4 REVIEW: Show Conviction

TO BE A GREAT LEADER:
1. Be Passionate About What You Are Doing
2. Get Through the Tough Times
3. Strengthen Confidence in Others

KEY CONCEPT
By believing completely in what you are doing, it enables you and those you lead to achieve outstanding results.

REALITY CHECK!
Often we face really tough times en route to where we want to go. To get through, as a leader you are asked to believe not only for yourself, but for others as well. And you just can't fake it. Conviction is real; people can feel it, and when you share your passion with them, they rally, too. It doesn't mean that there aren't moments of self-doubt. There are. But when you don't give up, when you commit and lead through the tough times by showing conviction, it helps others through as well.

Bring This Trait to Life
As different situations unfold, check in with yourself:

- Are you connected to that infectious passion that ensures you never give up on yourself?
- Do you overcome setbacks and enable those you are leading to overcome moments of doubt?
- Does your conviction spread to others?

LEADERS

Communicate Effectively

■ TRAIT 5

TRAIT 5:

Communicate Effectively

KEY CONCEPT

By creating an environment where direction is clear and opinions are freely shared, people are engaged and feel part of the process.

DEBBIE: The worst-case scenario that could happen when you are competing with a team of athletes on foreign soil is that one of them gets seriously injured. Unfortunately, that is exactly what happened at the World Aquatic Championships in Shanghai.

On the way back from the pool to the hotel, one of the athletes on the Canadian team realized that he had forgotten his camera. As most of us would react, he immediately wanted to return to the site to see if he could find it. Convincing the bus driver to pull over once passing through a busy tunnel, this athlete began to cross the street filled with traffic and was struck by a car. He was hit very hard, and was rendered completely unconscious and would remain so for many hours.

Communicating effectively is always important, but especially during a time of crisis. The Canadian officials had to manage a very difficult situation in the best way possible to make sure this horrible accident wasn't made worse by misinformation or alarming behavior. With the rest of the Canadian team still competing, and the health of one of their athletes at stake, a lot was on the line.

It was really important to make sure that the communication of the accident was given to the right people at the right time. The leadership took careful steps to make a plan to ensure there were no holes or gaps. Who would be responsible for delivering the various messages? When and what needed to be said to the parents? What needed to be communicated to the athletes and staff back at the host hotel? How could they best keep everyone calm and not let this terrible but isolated accident distract from the performance of the rest of the team? What message needed to be sent to the officials in China? Who would create the press release that would go back to Canada so they had control of what was said? Who would be the official spokesperson as the messages rolled out?

With their athlete in the best care possible at the hospital, and after deliberating carefully, the communication plan was executed smoothly and efficiently. What could have been a situation that became out of control was contained in the best way imaginable. The leaders also kept their internal communication flowing, making sure everyone was kept up to date and each person knew the key messages so the communication was clear and consistent to everyone.

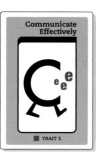

TO BE A GREAT LEADER:
1. Pay Attention to What, When, and How You Communicate
2. Notice the Reaction and Actions of Others
3. Keep Communication Flowing

1. Pay Attention to What, When, and How You Communicate

When we speak of the **WHAT**, we mean the information or message to be relayed. Be clear on what it is you are aiming to get across, and pay attention to the words you use. Language is powerful. Your words set the tone; how you use them will influence performance negatively or positively. Choose wisely. Consider also the quality versus the quantity of your communication. Some people talk a lot without really saying anything. What do you want to say? What are the best words to use to say it?

The **WHEN** refers to the timing of your communication. You can have a clear message delivered in a powerful way, but if the timing isn't right, you can fail to communicate effectively. Timing is everything, and wrong timing can lead to a distraction, to information falling on deaf ears, or worse, can negatively impact performance. You need to find the moment when your information can be taken in usefully.

The **HOW** means paying attention to the way you deliver the message. It is the tone, intonation, and manner in which the message is relayed. How you communicate the message can be verbal, reflected in the tone of voice, for example. However, often it is the non-verbal clues that speak the loudest. Notice how you communicate what you need to get across. How is your message being received?

It is the *right* message told at the *right* time the *right* way that makes for effective communication.

MARK: *A legendary communication disaster happened to one of the Olympic coaches who both Debbie and I know. In fact, Debbie was at a banquet when this national team coach confided in her that he was proud to have taken responsibility for his coaching mistakes. Admitting an error is honorable, but when you admit it is even more important. Like the famous expression, timing is everything.*

This particular coach recognized he had made a fundamental error in preparing his athletes to have their best performance at the Olympics. He mistimed the competition, realizing that his athletes would not be ready for the actual Games but would peak one week later instead. And he felt sick about it. So what did he do? He sat his athletes down two nights before the Olympics began and apologized to them. He wanted to let them know that he was taking the blame for the bad results that were about to happen when they competed. "I screwed up. You're not ready to race at your best. I am so sorry."

Not only was the timing of his message unbelievably bad, but the words he chose relayed the message that these athletes who had prepared their entire lives for this moment were not going to be ready to race well, no matter what. And, no surprise, they didn't. His words became a self-fulfilling prophecy.

LEADERS

The point here is to be aware of the words we are using and the time at which we say them, and to understand the impact they have on those we are leading. The wrong words at the wrong time limit possibilities; the right words at the right time expand them.

2. Notice the Reaction and Actions of Others

The meaning of the communication is found in the response that you get. A fundamental part of this trait is paying attention to what comes back to you. Listen to and observe how people are reacting to what you are saying to them. Make sure your message was taken as intended. Use your communication skills to ensure that you can support the efforts of your team. When the people you are leading appear to need something to help them improve, you must find the best possible way to get that message to them.

Information comes to us in different ways. Non-verbal language also gives us insight into what is really going on with those around us. The actions of others tell you whether or not they understood you. It is important to observe and listen carefully to what people are doing and telling you in order to evaluate how effectively you are communicating.

DEBBIE: I was brought in to work on communication skills with Peter, the director of software development in a large web design company. He had alienated many people, and one of his project managers went so far as to threaten to quit if she had to work with him anymore.

Peter explained how sometimes after just one conversation, people seemed to shut him out. He gave me an example. "I had been discussing some work that had been done for a client with an account manager. I told him that I couldn't believe the lack of quality in the work done to date. It was obvious someone hadn't been doing his or her job. That had been when the conversation halted, and after that our relationship hadn't been the same."

I asked Peter if he thought perhaps the account manager had taken what he said personally. "Maybe he felt what you said was slamming him for not paying attention to the quality of the work?" A little light went on in Peter's head. He said he'd never meant it like that, but he saw how it could be taken that way. I suggested one solution might be to say, "I can see lots of opportunity for making this site a lot better." What the person hears is "opportunity" and "better" as opposed to "lack of quality" and "[not] doing his or her job." There is a huge difference. Peter came to realize that communication was not just about getting the point across; it was equally important to understand how that message was received.

3. Keep Communication Flowing

Great leadership is about allowing information to flow. Your job is to create the environment where people can share their thoughts and ideas, where healthy debate can occur, and people ultimately feel their ideas and input are heard and valued.

When people are not afraid to speak up, say what they really think, and challenge others' ideas in a respectful way, you will know you've been successful. You will see that when people trust each other, they are far more engaged in their work, and expect more and give more of themselves. All of which are by-products of an open environment where communication flows freely.

MARK: *For over five years, I was the chair of a board that had major communication issues with the CEO. Instead of allowing information to flow, she tended to guard all of the portfolios to ensure that we were only hearing what she wanted us to hear. Information was only given one way. If anyone asked hard questions, she would fly off the handle, screaming that she wasn't being trusted, and sometimes even swearing at the board member who raised a concern. Needless to say, this created an incredibly toxic environment. One by one, I watched as my fellow board members closed down and gave up trying to communicate and understand what was going on with the organization. Many simply quit because they refused to be treated like this.*

In the daily operations of the organization, things were no different. If directors tried something new, they were humiliated in front of the management team. There was no room for ideas to flow; anyone wanting to suggest anything innovative or wanting to take a risk was essentially told to shut up, to listen to what the boss had to say, or leave. That was an option a remarkable number of employees decided to take. People became afraid of the reaction they would get from the leader if they did anything on their own. One by one, many of the directors stopped investing themselves in their departments; people became unmotivated and stopped caring about the outcome. In the course of five years, we lost six board members and five key management directors, and the project failed to reach its ultimate objectives. There were many factors, but the communication style of the leader certainly played an important part of the disappointing result.

■ TRAIT 5 REVIEW: Communicate Effectively

TO BE A GREAT LEADER:

1. Pay Attention to What, When, and How You Communicate
2. Notice the Reaction and Actions of Others
3. Keep Communication Flowing

KEY CONCEPT

By creating an environment where direction is clear and opinions are freely shared, people are engaged and feel part of the process.

REALITY CHECK!

Sometimes leaders are afraid to allow people to say what they think or to have two-way communication in case they hear what they don't want to hear. To avoid this, leaders sometimes close themselves off from giving and getting constructive criticism. Effectively communicating means creating the kind of environment where people aren't afraid to express themselves It enables ideas to flow and breakthroughs to happen.

Bring This Trait to Life

As different situations unfold, check in with yourself:

- Are you paying attention to what, when, and how you communicate?
- Do you take into consideration the feedback you are given, and apply it to make things better?
- Are you creating a trusting environment where high-level communication happens?

LEADERS

TRAIT 6:
Exemplify Excellence

KEY CONCEPT
By using the power of your example, you inspire
excellence in others.

MARK: *A top executive at one of the companies I worked with regularly brought his dog to work. It was a cute thing, and everyone loved him; this dog was like the company mascot.*

Soon, though, several other people started bringing their dogs to work, as well. As you walked into the main reception area, you would be greeted by a number of dogs, all jumping up on you. It was getting out of hand, so a memo went around telling everyone that dogs were no longer allowed in the workplace. This was no problem for the employees—until they realized that the rule didn't apply to the executive. He continued to bring his dog. Somehow, he was above the memo.

People were very annoyed and became quite cynical. In that single action of not following his own rules, this leader had lost all the credibility and trust of those he was leading. As drastic as it may sound, this incident was the beginning of the end for him.

Another leader potentially faced a similar fate, but managed to turn it around. He was a smoker, in a non-smoking office, and as he began to stay at the office after regular business hours, he started to break the rules and not go outside. Instead, he smoked in his office. At first, it went unnoticed, but soon some of the other people working late who were also smokers came to his office to join him. By the second week, he was being interrupted every few minutes with people coming by to smoke. He recognized that he had created the problem in the first place and decided he needed to take drastic action to change things. He quit smoking, and his office stopped being the smoking zone. The problem was solved. People still worked hard, and sometimes late, but the constant stopping for smoking breaks ended.

TO BE A GREAT LEADER:
1. Take an Honest Look in the Mirror
2. Be an Excellent Example
3. Shine the Light on Others

1. Take an Honest Look in the Mirror

For most of the Leader Traits, the focus has been on connecting others to their best. In the first part of this trait, we ask you to look at *yourself* and reflect on the kind of example *you* are setting. There are certain basic leadership qualities that are universally recognized.

Great leaders are:
- Trustworthy
- Supportive
- Respectful
- Good Listeners
- Consistently Positive
- Acting with Integrity
- Recognizing Others
- Approachable

At first glance, it is easy to say to yourself, "yes, I am all of these things." That is because, generally speaking, most good leaders *do* bring these qualities to life. The question becomes how often and how consistently? We usually don't put a lot of thought into how we *specifically* bring these qualities to life. It is fundamental as a leader that you are purposefully aligning your actions with these leadership qualities on a regular basis. Think about a specific time frame, like the past month, and how you have been with the people you lead. Ask yourself the following questions:

- How do I show trustworthiness for the people I lead on a day-to-day basis?
- How am I supportive?
- How do I treat them with respect?
- How do I listen well?
- Is my energy consistently positive?
- How are my actions in line with my words?
- How do I recognize the achievements of others?
- How am I approachable?

When you really stop and think about the above leadership qualities, which do you need to consciously make a point of doing better?

MARK: *If we don't hold up a mirror to ourselves, inevitably someone else will do it for us. When working with the International Olympic Committee, our mandate was to choose the best city possible for the best athletes of the world to have the best competition. But we became sidetracked taking gifts, wining and dining with the bigwigs, and letting our self-interest influence the process instead of doing our job properly. It was in the last city where we got busted.*

Nelson Mandela watched us getting organized for a photo with him after his presentation. We left the middle space for him, in between the oldest and most important members of the commission. When they called him to come in for the picture, Mr. Mandela went straight to the back, taking the youngest and most junior person on the commission to the middle place in the front that had been reserved for him, and then returned to take her spot in the back for the picture. "Ready for the photo," he said. Without saying a word, he showed us not only that we were all equal here, but also how out of synch we were with our own purpose.

LEADERS

2. Be an Excellent Example

As the leader, you set the stage for your environment. How you act will be a visual guide for those you lead. Your actions will ripple out and determine how those you are leading will, in turn, behave. Great leaders gain trust and respect from those they are leading by role modeling how they want them to be, in good times and bad.

It is easy to be graceful when things are going well. It is under pressure that you show people your true colors. What example are you setting by the way you are being when times are tough? Is there congruency between your words and actions? If someone were to walk into your environment, what would they notice or feel about it? Would they leave thinking to themselves that they would love to work there, or would they be running for the hills?

DEBBIE: A number of years ago, I was coaching a large group of swimmers and got very angry because no one was listening to me. Everyone was talking among themselves, interrupting, and arguing. I became so frustrated that I just walked out on them. I knew the moment I did it that it was absolutely the worst thing I could have done.

Would it be acceptable for them to walk out of a practice if they became frustrated?

My thinking behind my action was well intentioned. I wanted to do something drastic that would get them to start paying attention to me. The unintended result was that I got defiance and anger—not a good thing to have when you want world-class performance.

Beyond just setting a bad example, what does an action like that say at the subconscious level? Without even realizing it, these are some of the unintended messages I had sent out:

■ She is giving up on us. (*I created doubts in the people I was leading.*)
■ She doesn't think we're good enough. (*They lost belief in themselves.*)
■ She solves problems by getting mad and then leaving. (*I don't go the distance.*)
■ We'll never know when our leader will fly off the handle. (*I lost their trust.*)
■ If the leader can storm out of here, so can I. (*It is okay to give up.*)

Great role modeling has the power to build trust, gain credibility, earn respect, and create a productive environment. But it can have the opposite effect if we are not careful. As a leader, you must remember that you are onstage every day. People are watching everything you do, the way you see things, and how you behave. It all starts with your example. Great leaders inspire others to want to give their best because they don't want to let them down. That is being an excellent example. Give other people a good example to live up to in good and bad times. That is the sign of a great leader.

3. Shine the Light on Others

Success is the by-product of an encouraged person. Great leadership requires the ability to delight in others' excellence. You need to tell people when they are doing something well. Don't take them for granted. Let them know they are good at what they do. Recognition is hugely important. By pointing out people's good examples, you give others a standard to live up to, which often inspires even greater action.

Your job is to show that there is enough room in this world for everyone to excel. As a leader, when you regularly hold up others, be sure that another's good example doesn't mean that others don't feel they aren't also great at what they do. People will come to understand that there are no limits to the human capacity for excellence. When people really get this concept, they can be inspired and feed off of the greatness of each other.

MARK: *When I first started taking public speaking classes, the leader of our group did a perfect job at setting the stage for each of us to recognize that there was enough room for all of us in the class to be excellent.*

Each week, there was a small prize for the person who best exemplified a particular attribute in their presentations. You might expect that the class of 40 adults, largely from sales backgrounds, would be competitive with each other, but the exact opposite happened. As each week went by, we saw that every one of us was good at something and had valuable information to share with the group. Instead of fighting each other for the prizes, we encouraged each other. In the last weeks of the class, the shyest person had a breakthrough and wowed the entire room. She received a thunderous standing ovation from her peers. I have never forgotten that simple lesson that each of us is good at something, and if we can find a way to delight in the excellence of others, then at the same time we enable ourselves to delight in our own excellence.

LEADERS

■ TRAIT 6 REVIEW: Exemplify Excellence

TO BE A GREAT LEADER:

1. Take an Honest Look in the Mirror
2. Be an Excellent Example
3. Shine the Light on Others

KEY CONCEPT

By using the power of your example, you inspire excellence in others.

REALITY CHECK!

It is human nature to get envious and a bit jealous when people around us are doing well. At first, you celebrate with them, but if someone gets too much success, you somehow feel that says something bad about you. So, you start looking at them differently, focusing on their faults, and secretly enjoying their mishaps. Great leaders know how to avoid this pitfall. By being an excellent example and celebrating the many good things in different people around them, you remind people that we are all pretty great in our own way, and someone else's success can reflect our own capacity for excellence.

Bring This Trait to Life

As different situations unfold, check in with yourself:

- When you hold the mirror up to yourself, is there congruence between what you say and what you do?
- Do you celebrate excellence in others?
- Does the power of your example inspire excellence in others?

Embrace Contradictions

■ TRAIT 7

TRAIT 7:

Embrace Contradictions

KEY CONCEPT

By being open to various possibilities in any given situation, you find what works even if that appears to contradict what you have done before.

MARK: *I have been involved in the Olympic movement for a long time. I was an athlete for sixteen years, and had gone on to become an executive board member of Toronto's Olympic bid, part of the athletes' commission for the International Aquatic Federation, as well as being a member of the Canadian Olympic Committee. Although I was still deeply committed to making a difference within the international sport scene, there came a moment when I seemed to completely contradict myself by stepping down from all of my involvements. How was leaving going to matter? Wasn't the best way to contribute to stay within?*

Under most circumstances, this might have held true. But following the Salt Lake City scandal, when deep-seated corruption within the Olympic movement made headlines around the world, there was an opportunity to face the serious problems and make a change for the better. Unfortunately, the leadership at that time was unwilling to take any personal responsibility or to face the situation honestly. Looking at all of the solutions available at that time, leaving seemed to be the best option for me to actually take some meaningful actions.

Starting with a couple of athletes and corporate supporters from Canada, and growing quickly to become an international grassroots campaign of advocates and athletes from around the world, we created Olympic Advocates Together Honorably (OATH), an organization that put pressure to reform from the outside. We were accused by many of trying to destroy the Olympic movement, but that wasn't our intention at all. As legendary swimmer John Naber put it, "We don't want to take over the running of international sport. We don't want a piece of the pie. We just want to make sure the pie tastes as good as the recipe intended it to." Even though we appeared to be contradicting ourselves by speaking against the Olympic leaders, our actions were driven from a place of values, namely how much we cared about preserving all that was good within the movement.

In the end, our group created a 93-page comprehensive report giving an overview of what was necessary to move toward an ethical foundation for Olympic reform. Interestingly, there were many people on the inside who were change-minded, and this report gave them the leverage to push some of the reform agenda forward. It was the combination of the people on the inside and what was being done on the outside that in the end helped shape the reform process.

TO BE A GREAT LEADER:
1. Accept the Nature of Paradox
2. Master the Art and Science of Leadership
3. Respect Core Values and Provide Rationale

1. Accept the Nature of Paradox

Extreme ideas, seemingly in opposition, can work brilliantly together. The following groupings are just a few examples of contradictions that we face putting ideas into action. Among them, there are no wrong or right statements, just notions from opposite ends of the spectrum to be used in different circumstances, depending on the situation.

Take a risk.
Be cautious.

Plan meticulously.
Go with the flow.

Be patient.
Go now!

Be consistent.
Change it up.

Use logic.
Follow your gut.

Work hard.
Have fun.

Don't compromise.
Be flexible.

The secret is to find what works most effectively in any given situation. There is no absolute right or wrong because there never is just one way to get something done. There may be one outcome you are striving for, but there are always several different possibilities to take you there. It is up to you to decide what is the best way forward in your particular circumstance. Do what works best with the people you are leading, even if that appears to contradict what you have done before.

2. Master the Art and Science of Leadership

We believe you can read every book on leadership, develop every skill set, understand rationally all the steps necessary to become a leader and still not have what it takes. This is because leadership is also about ambiguities, perceptions, and feelings. Take communication as an example. It is the combination of knowing the right words to use (the What) with the right timing (the When) that makes for great communication.

LEADERS

Leadership encompasses two seemingly contradictory concepts. On one hand, we have the practical, rational, pragmatic, step-by-step approach that we call the "science" of leadership. On the other hand, we have the concept that is harder to quantify. It is awareness, your gut feeling, the instinct that something is working or not that we call the "art" of leadership. It is the effective integration of these two seemingly contradictory elements that creates great leaders.

Different things work for different people—we are not all the same. Great leaders are able to adapt what they do to access the full potential of each individual they lead.

Sometimes that will mean intervening.
Other times it will mean standing back.

Sometimes it will mean giving feedback immediately.
Other times it should be delayed.

Sometimes you will give control.
Other times you will take it.

Sometimes you will listen.
Other times you will talk.

Great leaders know what to do and when to do it, and know it for themselves and others, too.

DEBBIE: I have had the opportunity to observe an up-and-coming coach as part of my mentoring responsibilities. Watching him in different situations, I noticed that he tended to go to yelling as his primary way of communicating with his athletes when he got frustrated. After observing a training session, I asked him what he was trying to get across, and showed him that yelling might not be the best way to do it. He agreed and worked on alternative, more effective ways of giving feedback to his athletes, especially in the heat of the moment of competition.

Many months later, I was there when once again he was yelling at his team. Although I would typically never condone this kind of behavior, in this particular instance it was the exact right thing to do. His athletes needed a jolt, and the best way to do that was to yell at them. Afterwards,

I sat with the coach and told him I liked the way he had handled the situation. "But I thought you didn't like it when I yell?" he asked. And usually I don't. But that is the nuance of leadership, knowing what to do when, and determining what is the right thing to do in any particular moment, even if it seems to contradict what you have said and done before.

3. Respect Core Values and Provide Rationale

You may be willing to do whatever works, but what should never be compromised are your values. Let them guide the process. That being said, values are one thing, rules and regulations are another, and over time these can become outdated. Sometimes you might continue to follow them just because you always have. If you do this, you run the risk of cementing yourself in obsolete rules and you will inevitably get stuck. As leader, you may need to contradict what has been done in the past to find a new and even better way forward, even if that means challenging established rules and regulations.

When embracing contradictions, it is very important to be clear on why you are doing what you are doing, and how that relates back to the larger objective. You must be able to clearly identify the rationale behind making the choices that you do.

It can be confusing if you are doing one thing one day, and then take an entirely different approach the next. It can open the door for distrust. People might not know how to read you. Be careful. If someone asks why you are doing something that seems like a contradiction and you respond, "Because I say so," chances are they won't buy in. If you are clear about why you are doing what you are doing, then people will support you. They will see that no matter what you do, you are coming from a place of looking at what will work best for them and the organization.

MARK: *I was part of a company whose leader had an unfortunate habit of saying one thing one day, and then doing a complete 180-degree turn the next. People never knew what to expect. You'd come in on Monday and be his best friend, come in Tuesday and he wouldn't even acknowledge you were there. He'd tell the team one day to focus on growing the business in Europe. Three days later, he would be angry because the team wasn't working on the American market. He continually contradicted himself.*

LEADERS

Slowly, the directors lost all of their confidence in him. They didn't want to bother investing in what he asked of them because they knew they would be asked to do something completely different as soon as they started down one path. The problem was that their leader was constantly in reactionary mode, not acting from a place of purpose that people could rally behind, but basing his strategy on a whim. He constantly contradicted himself without any rationale, and wasn't making good decisions for the team. Eventually, the respect and solidarity of his people evaporated. His results fell well short of the intended outcome, mostly because in the end, he was surrounded by yes people and not the best people.

LEADERS

■ TRAIT 7 REVIEW: Embrace Contradictions

TO BE A GREAT LEADER:

1. Accept the Nature of Paradox
2. Master the Art and Science of Leadership
3. Respect Core Values and Provide Rationale

KEY CONCEPT

By being open to various possibilities in any given situation, you find what works even if that appears to contradict what you have done before.

REALITY CHECK!

Often as leaders, we are fearful of being seen as contradictory. You don't want to be known for constantly changing your mind or going a different route on a whim. In order to counteract this, you might become more rigid in your approach. You don't want to appear like you are losing control. Embracing contradictions means staying open to what works best in any given situation and letting go of that fear. It enables you to make the best decisions possible and move things forward.

Bring This Trait to Life

As different situations unfold, check in with yourself:

- Are you seeing different possibilities in challenging situations?
- Do you make decisions based on what works instead of what is right or wrong?
- Are your decisions consistent with your values?

LEADERS

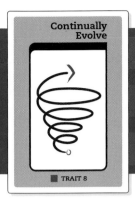

TRAIT 8:
Continually Evolve

> ### KEY CONCEPT
> By creating a dynamic environment where the bar
> is constantly being raised, excellence is fostered
> and outstanding results happen.

DEBBIE: Our story ends back where it started. Mark and I began our personal and professional journey together when he had become complacent and stopped evolving. Ranked second in the world, he made the mistake that so many of us do. He had thought he had it all figured out, and that if he simply kept doing what he was doing, then he would remain on top of his game. That way of thinking caught up with him and forced him to change in order to get to the next level, which, in his case, was to become a champion and win Olympic gold.

In a sense, that was where this book was first born. For 20 years, I had refined my own approach as a coach who could lead synchronized swimmers to excellence, and working with Mark helped me further evolve by applying those ideas to a completely new and different environment. That first year Mark and I worked together, we would spend countless hours exploring the ideas that would one day become this book.

Over 10 years ago, we had started to write a book together, but at that particular juncture, the timing wasn't right for us. The ideas were all there, but we needed more time to evolve, to apply these concepts in different ways with others to further clarify for ourselves what the fundamentals were. I went on to work with businesses, and eventually came back to the sport system, leading a team that reviewed all of the summer and winter sports to connect them to higher levels of performance. Mark went on to work within the political side of international sport, and then to television, speaking and leading social change movements. Even though we weren't officially writing or working together, further exploring the ideas we had started as coach and athlete became the basis of our long-standing friendship.

This book has been a testament to the idea of continually evolving. When we came back together to make another attempt at writing, the timing was absolutely right. But the book changed form dozens of times from when we began to the product you are holding in your hands now. The fundamental ideas never changed, but how we expressed them went through constant refinement. We started with baby steps, and once one trait came together, it gave us the confidence to move to the next. Over the course of many, many months, we gained the momentum needed to finally turn those independent ideas into a book. Looking back to the experience that brought us together close to twenty years ago, we had to apply that same thinking to evolve to where we are today.

LEADERS

TO BE A GREAT LEADER:
1. Build Momentum
2. Have High Expectations
3. Encourage a Culture of Improvement

1. Build Momentum

Success breeds further success. The small wins you have with those you are leading fuels their belief in themselves and what they are a part of, which makes it possible to achieve better and better results. What you do today impacts what you are able to do tomorrow. When you have a small success, the bar can be raised a bit higher the next day, and then the next, and so on.

There are a couple of misconceptions about achieving great results. The first is that in order to achieve fantastic outcomes, huge things have to happen. In reality, it is the small incremental steps that eventually add up to make the big difference. Over time, the accumulation of these small successes leads to world-class performance and outstanding results. The second misconception is that every day has to be better than the last. It doesn't work like that. Continually evolving is also about persevering through the hard times and facing setbacks. A great leader has the ability to find some small success even if the day is a disaster. Learning from what is not working to find what will work is what keeps momentum building.

MARK: *A colleague of mine was a junior account manager for an ad agency. For a long time, she was very excited about work and the challenges it presented, but eventually she found herself getting bored and restless as her work became routine. Her job was no longer stimulating and she started to develop a bad attitude, losing the momentum that had once made her great.*

Luckily, she had a wise boss who understood that he needed to provide her with greater challenges or risk losing her. He took a chance and put her in as the lead of a huge account for a new client, raising the bar for her and creating a new momentum. She faced some tough times along the way, but rising to this challenge stimulated her again, and she turned her deteriorating interest and success around. Her boss had taken a calculated risk, but he believed in her ability to do the job and knew she had to grow and be challenged. This helped her evolve to a new level. The risk turned out to be a good one. The campaign that she created for the client went on to win numerous national and international awards.

2. Have High Expectations

People live up to what your expectations are of them. If you expect too little from people, that is likely what you will get. Never underestimate the capacity of those you lead to be great. They can accomplish whatever is set out for them.

LEADERS

The question is, how do you continually set the bar higher without overwhelming people, or making your team feel like no matter what they do, it is never good enough? This is where the "art" of leadership comes in to play—using your awareness to increase expectations in a way that is empowering and motivating to those you lead. It is about finding those coachable moments when you know someone is in a place to be challenged to be even better. Timing is critical in knowing when to raise the bar and by how much. Done poorly, people feel that you are never satisfied, which translates into unmotivated people who limit their own potential. Done well, raising the bar engages and challenges people to evolve to a higher level.

Great leaders constantly have high expectations for themselves and others. As you raise expectations, it is crucial that you also provide the training and tools necessary to support that. You can't expect performance and results to get better if you haven't provided the resources necessary to get people to the next level. Appropriate training and resources go hand in hand with higher expectations.

DEBBIE: I recall training for the World Aquatic Championships at the University of Toronto pool. One day, our consultant from Sport Canada came to have a meeting with me. Unfortunately, the day he chose to observe, we were having a lot of trouble with our execution. It was the end of a high-volume training period and everyone was tired. Following the workout, I met with the consultant.

"What are your performance goals for the World Championships?" he asked.

"Three gold medals," was my reply.

There was a long pause, and then he countered, "Are you sure you want to commit to that? It's a bit of a long shot, don't you think?"

"I know it's a big stretch, but we believe we can achieve it," I said.

"Okay, but you don't have to say that. If you tell me you want three gold medals and we put it down on paper and you don't achieve it, that's going to look like you failed," he said.

"And we will have failed," I replied. "I believe we can win three and I don't want to lower that expectation."

"Well, judging from what I saw today, you'll be lucky if you win one," he said.

I countered, "The goal is three gold medals and we're not settling for anything less. We've raised the bar and are committed to it. I don't want to play it safe."

A month later, we won all three events at the World Aquatic Championships. There were some nail-biting moments for sure, but I don't think it would have happened if we hadn't clearly stated that that was our goal and we were willing to take it public. Our expectations were high, the training program that could get the athletes to a level that matched our expectations was provided, and the results followed suit.

3. Encourage a Culture of Improvement

It is human nature to resist change, but whether we like it or not, the world around us is constantly evolving. What is accepted as a great result today might not be so good tomorrow. That is why it is so important to keep your expectations high. How do you challenge others not to become complacent?

A large part of that is creating an environment that values innovation, where people feel safe to take risks and make mistakes. Often, the way we evolve is through trial and error. If you expect perfection every time, there is no room to explore. People get paralyzed with fear, stuck doing what might have worked at one time, but not being able to adapt and evolve to find what is needed to work now. By allowing people to take risks and make mistakes, you create a learning culture. People know it is okay to make mistakes as long as they learn from them.

Ultimately, your job is to create the environment for excellence to happen. To ensure you are doing that, make sure you evaluate yourself from time to time. Check in with yourself as it is easy to get complacent, especially when things are going well. Critical self-reflection is fundamental to ongoing success. Evaluate your actions and challenge yourself to be even better. That is what great leaders do.

LEADERS

■ TRAIT 8 REVIEW: Continually Evolve

TO BE A GREAT LEADER:

1. Build Momentum
2. Have High Expectations
3. Encourage a Culture of Improvement

KEY CONCEPT

By creating a dynamic environment where the bar is constantly being raised, excellence is fostered and outstanding results happen.

REALITY CHECK!

There is a really fine line between continuing to do what you've done because it is working, and knowing when to evolve to do things in a different and better way. You do not want to constantly change things that are working, and at the same time you do not want to wait until they don't work. By creating an environment where people can make mistakes—and they will—change will always be welcome. Continually evolving creates a culture that is always challenging itself to become better.

Bring This Trait to Life

As different situations unfold, check in with yourself:

- Are you building on small successes with those you are leading?
- Is the bar being raised with expectations set higher?
- Do people feel supported to take risks in a dynamic environment?

LEADERS

KEY CONCEPT SYNOPSIS
THE LEADER TRAITS
Creating Champion Organizations and Teams

 The greater your awareness, the greater your capacity to act effectively as a leader.

 By creating an environment where direction is clear and opinions are freely shared, people are engaged and feel part of the process.

 By capturing people's imagination with clear objectives and roles, you inspire everyone to do their part in making it happen.

 By using the power of your example, you inspire excellence in others.

 By bringing together the right people, an inexplicable energy is created that produces winning results much greater than any one individual's contribution.

 By being open to various possibilities in any given situation, you can find what works even if that appears to contradict what you have done before.

 By believing completely in what you are doing, it enables you and those you lead to achieve outstanding results.

 By creating a dynamic environment where the bar is constantly being raised, excellence is fostered and winning results happen.

LEADERS

LEADER TRAITS—SELF-ASSESSMENT

Before moving on in this book, take the time to complete this quick, simple evaluation tool. See which Leader Traits need more work than others and invest some time in them.

Rate yourself on a scale of 1 to 4:

1 = Strongly Disagree, 2 = Disagree, 3 = Agree, 4 = Strongly Agree

Leader Trait		Personal Life	Professional Life
1. Be Aware I consciously think about how I can frame my thoughts to be more empowering for myself and those I lead.	A⁺	1 2 3 4	1 2 3 4
Actions to Improve			
I help those I am leading be aware of their empowering and limiting thoughts, and how they can use them to create winning results.		1 2 3 4	1 2 3 4
Actions to Improve			
2. Have Purpose Everyone on the team clearly knows what the objective is and their role in it.	☆	1 2 3 4	1 2 3 4
Actions to Improve			
I have a clear plan, including actions and benchmarks for each person involved.		1 2 3 4	1 2 3 4
Actions to Improve			

Leader Trait		Personal Life	Professional Life
3. Create Synergy I have the right people in the right roles.		1 2 3 4	1 2 3 4
Actions to Improve			
The team is performing at the high-performance level.		1 2 3 4	1 2 3 4
Actions to Improve			
4. Show Conviction I believe completely in what we are doing and the objectives we have established.		1 2 3 4	1 2 3 4
Actions to Improve			
I am able to lead everyone through the tough times and instil confidence in what we are doing.		1 2 3 4	1 2 3 4
Actions to Improve			

Leader Trait		Personal Life	Professional Life
5. Communicate Effectively My words and actions communicate the points I want to get across.		1 2 3 4	1 2 3 4
Actions to Improve			
I have created an open environment where ideas and feedback are freely exchanged.		1 2 3 4	1 2 3 4
Actions to Improve			
6. Exemplify Excellence The example I set is the one I want others to follow.		1 2 3 4	1 2 3 4
Actions to Improve			
I often hold up others as examples of excellence.		1 2 3 4	1 2 3 4
Actions to Improve			

Leader Trait	Personal Life	Professional Life
7. Embrace Contradictions I look for what will work in any given situation, as opposed to what I have always done before.	1 2 3 4	1 2 3 4
Actions to Improve		
I am able to provide rationale for all decisions and actions that I make.	1 2 3 4	1 2 3 4
Actions to Improve		
8. Continually Evolve I continuously raise the bar to create a high performing environment for all.	1 2 3 4	1 2 3 4
Actions to Improve		
I maximize small successes to create positive momentum.	1 2 3 4	1 2 3 4
Actions to Improve		

LEADERS

The Legacy Traits

Championing a
Meaningful Way of Life

Each of the Legacy Traits has a graphic icon highlighted in orange to help support the key ideas found within.

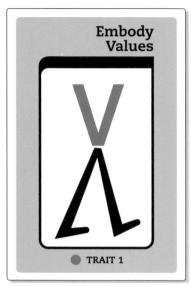

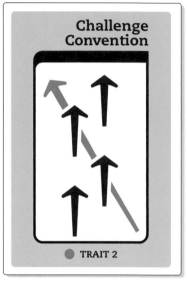

TRAIT ONE:
The V on the stick legs reminds us to bring our values to life.

TRAIT TWO:
The one arrow crossing the others represents the importance to sometimes go against popular thinking.

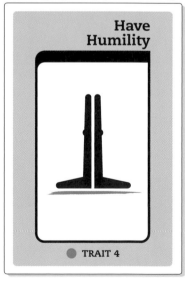

TRAIT THREE:
The plus sign (+) reminds us of the opportunity we all have to make a positive impact on others.

TRAIT FOUR:
The knobby-kneed figure reminds us to stay humble and grounded.

Use all eight icons as visual reminders of the key concepts and ideas within each of the Legacy Traits.

TRAIT FIVE:
The smiling face in motion represents the kindness with which we can move through life.

TRAIT SIX:
The globe simply represents the larger world we are all a part of.

TRAIT SEVEN:
The alarm clock reminds us to wake up to this moment.

TRAIT EIGHT:
The check in the star represents that you can make things happen for yourself and others.

Your *Great Traits* **Champion's Journey** concludes with the Legacy Traits. The final part of this book ensures that while you are achieving and leading people to great things, you pay close attention to the larger impact you are making on the world around you. None of us acts or lives in silos. The Legacy Traits, symbolized by the circle, help you make sure your words, actions, and spirit ripple out and positively affect others long into the future.

For us, legacy happens by example, and you can learn how to use that to make a lasting win for yourself and others. Every single one of us has the possibility to impact thousands and thousands of people we come into contact with. Little seemingly incidental actions taken by you can leave a lasting impression on others. So, just as you can learn fundamental ideas that support you being a better salesperson or parent, so too can you learn basic ideas that help you be a better person by considering the future and how your actions can positively impact it.

The *Great Traits Champion's Journey* began with you taking a *me*-centered focus in Achievers to build the foundation to personally succeed. Then it shifted to you taking a *we*-centered focus in Leaders, so that both you and those you lead could accomplish great things. In this final section, the focus broadens again, asking you to look at how you can use your experience largely for the benefit of *all*.

Of all the sections, this is the one that has changed the most in this second edition. When we first released *The Great Traits of Champions*, we were reluctant to prescribe *how* to leave a legacy, and instead looked generally at being more conscious of *what* legacy you inevitably leave. In this edition, we approach Legacy with much clearer learning objectives.

We have found in the years between publications that the ideas and learning that are laid out in the Achiever and Leader sections come together to create something new in Legacy. You will see how all of the traits are built upon to create this final section of the *Champion's Journey*.

Each Legacy Trait begins with a quick anecdote of a global figure that we believe brings that particular trait to life. Then, we identify a key concept that describes what we mean for that trait. Next, we have learning objectives and anecdotes where you will see how the skills you have already mastered in the Achiever and Leader sections come together to create new concepts that are impactful, positive, and beneficial for others. At the end, there is a Review section with a summary and questions to make sure you are consciously maximizing your legacy.

Every single one of us leaves a legacy. By waking up to that reality, you can begin to consciously decide which actions to take that will have a positive influence. This is what the Legacy Traits are all about.

The final step of your *Champion's Journey* happens here and now.

Have fun!

Embody
Values

TRAIT 1

TRAIT 1:
Embody Values

A Legendary Example of This Trait

*Kim Phuc is one of the most famous subjects of a photograph the world
has ever seen. Caught in war, she was the girl in the middle of the road,
burned so severely she would need to stay in the hospital for 14 months,
an unforgettable image of the Vietnam tragedy. Named a UNESCO Goodwill Ambassador 20 years later, she now values peace and forgiveness.
Her personal bravery enabled her, on the way back to Cuba following
her honeymoon, to get off the plane during a refuelling stop in Canada
and ask for political asylum. Today she is part of a strong community, has
a husband and a family—and has found peace within to be able to speak
out through the work she does. She was asked to give a speech at the U.S.
Vietnam Veterans Memorial in Washington, DC, on Veterans' Day, and
briefly met a man who was part of the team that ordered the bomb to be
dropped on her. She listened intensely to his story, and then she forgave
him. Kim Phuc leaves a legacy everywhere she goes by embodying the
values she believes in.*

TO LEAVE A LEGACY:
1. Know Your Values
2. Let Your Values Drive Your Actions
3. Keep Yourself in Check

1. Know Your Values

It is important to know what you value. There is no right or wrong here. Some values include freedom, order, adventure, achievement, friendship, pleasure, privacy, wealth, trust, and loyalty. What we are asking of you is to consider which are important to you. If someone who knows you were asked about you, what values would he or she say you embody? What are the values that drive your life? Once you are clear on that, it becomes much easier to make decisions and to act in a way that is consistent and congruent with who you are, and how you want to be remembered.

MARK: *The Vancouver 2010 Winter Olympic Games were regarded as a huge success, and much of that achievement can be credited to the CEO of VANOC, John Furlong. For the seven years leading up to the Games, as his team grew to include thousands, each person joining the organizing committee was guided by a clear set of values that were laid out by John early in the process. Teamwork was value #1, then trust, excellence, creativity, and sustainability. In John's own words, "Our values would be so ingrained that we would know instantly if something was off with a potential business partner." This clear identification of values gave the organization and every person in it a clear foundation from which to make decisions. John envisioned the Olympic Games as a vehicle to improve the fabric of Canadian society, and his legacy came from demonstrating that the delivery of the Olympics built on solid values can be a true nation builder.*

2. Let Your Values Drive Your Actions

The Legacy Traits build on the learning from the Achiever and Leader Traits to create something lasting and powerful. In Achiever Trait 4: Act Effectively, you were asked to align your actions with your goals. This first Legacy Trait builds on that idea and asks you to align your actions not only with your goals, but also with your values. Getting to the goal is one thing; who you are when you get there is just as important.

3. Keep Yourself in Check

Leader Trait 6: Exemplify Excellence asked you to look in the mirror to see how you were being for those you were leading. This trait, Embody Values, builds on that by asking you to think about who you are and how you live those values in your daily life. Are you acting in a way that is in line with your values? If not, make a change so that there is congruency between what you value and the way you act.

DEBBIE: I have always valued my freedom. When I first began coaching, there wasn't necessarily a lot of money to be made, but my career choice gave me independence and autonomy, both of which were really important to me. Toward the end of my coaching career when I was considering what to do next, I was presented with many different options. One particular corporate position was very tempting, but even though I had the possibility of making a lot of money and having security, I knew that the trade-off was that I would lose my freedom. I had to listen to myself and not get tempted by what seemed like a great opportunity, but was not in line with what I valued.

LEGACY

● TRAIT 1 REVIEW: Embody Values

TO LEAVE A LEGACY:
1. Know Your Values
2. Let Your Values Drive Your Actions
3. Keep Yourself in Check

KEY CONCEPT

Your values act as a compass that guides your decision making and shows people who you are.

REALITY CHECK!

Many of us aren't very clear about what we really value. Take some time to check out your values and start to get in tune with them. It is hard to embody something you aren't aware of. When you are clear on what you stand for, you are able to stand for what you value.

Bring This Trait to Life

To make a difference, consider the following:

- What values are important to you?
- How do your values show up in your day-to-day living?
- Are there better ways you can champion the values you believe in?

LEGACY

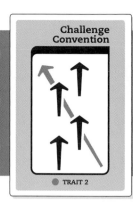

TRAIT 2:
Challenge Convention

KEY CONCEPT
Having the courage to challenge the status quo often leads to breakthroughs for yourself and others.

A Legendary Example of This Trait

Roger Bannister became a track and field legend. While at Oxford, he drew attention from the media and school officials. He chose to forego the 1948 Olympics for his medical studies, and then in 1952, although he was the British champion, he came fourth at the Olympics in his best event, the 1500-meter race. The media scorned him, so he set out to prove them wrong. To redeem himself, he decided to break the world record for the mile and be the first person under the four-minute barrier. Although still a full-time medical student with only 45 minutes a day to train, he knew he could do it despite what others thought. On May 6, 1954, at Oxford University, a 25-year-old Roger Bannister made history by running the mile in 3 minutes 59.4 seconds. Within weeks, another runner had broken the record. But Roger Bannister broke it first, and by doing so, enabled many others to see themselves doing it, too.

TO LEAVE A LEGACY:
1. Know the Status Quo
2. Question When Necessary
3. Find a New Way When Required

1. Know the Status Quo

The status quo is simply reflective of the way things have been *and* continue to be. It is what the collective group thinks. It doesn't make it right or even truthful—it is what the majority of people assume, and that influences how they act. By keeping things the same, you stay in your comfort zone. You become so comfortable, you don't even want to consider changing something. Pay attention. Before you can challenge convention, you have to know what it is.

2. Question When Necessary

Tradition, rules, and the law all serve a purpose, and can be very valuable. But if people never challenged what came before them, society would never move forward. Achiever Trait 2: Expand Your Perspective asked you to notice what you notice due to selective awareness. This Trait, Challenge Convention, builds on that idea to question where society's selective aware-ness has led to limitations that need to be challenged for progress to occur.

DEBBIE: When she was 58 years old, Mary Boon entered a fun walk known as the Santa Shuffle in her community. Enjoying the experience of being outdoors and walking with friends, Mary decided she would like to become a runner. At a time when many begin to exercise less, Mary decided to embark on a long-distance running career, something that even most young people don't consider.

It wasn't always easy. In her first 10 km race, Mary forgot to drink water, struggled to finish, and showed up at the end of the course green in the face. But she had a taste of what it was to be a runner, and she liked

LEGACY

it. She ran another 10 km. Eventually, a half-marathon. Then another. As training and racing kept going well, Mary ran a marathon. Then another. Mary began setting records when she was in her sixties. Running had literally helped her find her stride.

At 72 years old, Mary joined thousands of other runners, mostly younger, at that start of the Boston Marathon. Her friends and family were there when she came to Heartbreak Hill, named such because of its location at the 21-mile mark of the course. As she approached, something wasn't right. Mary said she had hurt her shoulder a bit from high-fiving so many other runners, and she was paying for it in her hip. It didn't matter. In the next hour she crossed the finish line of the Boston Marathon, completing a dream of a lifetime (and with her perfect pedicure intact!). Most of us don't think it is possible to run a marathon. Mary challenged what society thought was possible for a woman of her age, and paved the way for others, too.

3. Find a New Way When Required

In considering different possibilities, new and better ways forward can emerge. Leader Trait 4: Show Conviction asked you to believe completely in what you are doing in order to lead others to breakthroughs. Challenging conventional wisdom requires a similar strength and leads to unveiling limitations in group thinking so that new and better ways of doing things can be developed. Without a challenge, we naturally fall into ruts. We need to get out of our comfort zones and make a change for the better.

MARK: *Since its founding in 1945, the United Nations had never touched the issue of sexual orientation. Even though much progress had been made in many countries, it was still not illegal to imprison or even execute gay individuals in many countries around the world. That changed in December 2008 when the Government of France introduced a declaration to decriminalize homosexuality to the General Assembly of the United Nations in New York City.*

I was invited to witness this historic occasion, and at the event after the vote had been taken, I was called upon to share my story. The little red light in front of me went on, and I quietly prayed my voice wouldn't betray how nervous I was. Even though there was much resistance to the declaration, I knew how important it was to put a human face to

LEGACY

the challenges gay people faced. It would take over two years, but finally in 2011, the United Nations Human Rights Council passed a resolution calling for a report on the situation of gay citizens worldwide. Sexual orientation was finally on the formal agenda.

● TRAIT 2 REVIEW: Challenge Convention

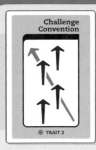

TO LEAVE A LEGACY:
1. Know the Status Quo
2. Question When Necessary
3. Find a New Way When Required

KEY CONCEPT

Having the courage to challenge the status quo often leads to breakthroughs for yourself and others.

REALITY CHECK!

Often, we are afraid to go against the grain because of what we fear the consequences might be. We could get hurt, look foolish, or get in trouble. Challenging convention enables us to find ways of doing things that are better than before and that often inspire others at the same time.

Bring This Trait to Life

To make a difference, consider the following:

- When have you gotten stuck blindly accepting the status quo?
- Can you champion yourself and others to find better ways of doing things?
- What different actions can you take that challenge you to be better?

LEGACY

Influence
Wisely

TRAIT 3

Influence Wisely

KEY CONCEPT

Recognize the impact you have with your life by sharing
your wisdom, experience, and knowledge with others.

A Legendary Example of This Trait

*Anita Roddick was best known for founding The Body Shop. She was
trained as a teacher, married and opened a restaurant and a hotel, and
worked for the United Nations where she traveled extensively and met
people from many different cultures. The Body Shop, founded in 1976,
always had an edge of social responsibility. Products were not tested on
animals, and recycling made practical sense. Those simple ideas led to
over 77 million customers a year. She cared deeply about people, especially disenfranchised and forgotten children. She founded Children on the
Edge (COTE) as a response to the orphaned and disadvantaged children
in Eastern Europe and Asia. Tragically, in February 2007, she revealed
that she had contracted Hepatitis C, and she died later that year. Anita
Roddick used her life to make a difference on every front for other people.*

Influence Wisely

i

TRAIT 3

TO LEAVE A LEGACY:
1. Embrace Who You Are
2. Be Willing to Share
3. Find the Best Way to Influence

1. Embrace Who You Are

Who you are is an accumulation of all of your experiences—and the knowledge and wisdom that has come with them. We often underestimate the meaning of that. Accept the significance of your own history, whatever it is. The value of your life experience is enormous.

DEBBIE: I have a friend who is now in her sixties, and as she has gotten older has found aging difficult to accept. Part of the problem is the way she looks, but the larger challenge is how she feels. As she watches new generations come behind her, she struggles with the notion of feeling irrelevant at this point in her life.

The most important thing to her is to feel like she is relevant, current, and can make a contribution in a meaningful way. She feels like she has to do something new and different with the next generation to make this happen. The irony is that she doesn't see just how much she has to offer simply by embracing her own life and valuing the experience she has accumulated. Instead of looking outside of herself for an opportunity to be current, she simply needs to look within her own history and embrace it. In sharing her knowledge and wisdom with others, she makes herself relevant, as those following in her footsteps can learn from her vast experiences.

2. Be Willing to Share

Everybody has influence, but how do *you* use it? You can manipulate situations for your own benefit, always putting yourself first, but there is not much of a legacy in that. In Achiever Trait 8: Generate Enthusiasm, we asked you to share your excitement about what you were doing to get others involved. In this Legacy Trait, we ask you to share your experience,

LEGACY

knowledge, and wisdom selflessly with others to move them forward. This is about you, and at the same time, not about you. Sharing doesn't necessarily mean people will do what you did. But it does give them another experience to consider, and that is invaluable.

3. Find the Best Way to Influence

Whether it is peer to peer, one generation to the next, or one culture to another, there are many ways to positively influence each other. Influencing wisely doesn't necessarily mean being "touchy feely." It might be tough love. In Leader Trait 1: Be Aware, we asked you to become aware of how your thoughts and beliefs impact those you lead. In this Legacy Trait, we build on that idea to consciously find the right time and way to share your experiences in order to positively impact those around you.

MARK: *In 1998, I got a call from my dad with the worst possible news. He had been diagnosed with melanoma cancer and was to begin chemotherapy immediately. It was a very difficult time, to say the least. At first he seemed to be completely weakened by his disease, but as he got closer to the end of the first round of treatment, he actually seemed to regain some strength. I was living on the other side of the country at that time, and traveled back and forth as much as possible to be with him.*

During one of his next rounds of chemotherapy, a nurse at the hospital approached me to tell me she was very sorry that our family was going through this difficult experience. When she found out I was going to head back home soon, she gently squeezed my arm, looked me in the eyes, and said, "Spend as much time as you can with him right now." Thanks to the way she handled the situation, I understood I had very limited time to be with my dad. Her words influenced me to be there for the remaining weeks before he died.

● TRAIT 3 REVIEW: Influence Wisely

TO LEAVE A LEGACY:

1. Embrace Who You Are
2. Be Willing to Share
3. Find the Best Way to Influence

KEY CONCEPT

Recognize the impact you have with your life by sharing your wisdom, experience, and knowledge with others.

REALITY CHECK!

We often underestimate our own experience and the wisdom we have gained, and don't even think to share it. Who do I think I am to speak up? To share something? But often we don't say what is obvious to us because we assume others know it. By wisely sharing our experience and perspective, we positively influence those around us.

Bring This Trait to Life

To make a difference, consider the following:

- What are some situations where you can positively influence others?
- What unique experience can you share with others to help move them forward?
- How are people around you influencing you?

TRAIT 4:
Have Humility

> ### KEY CONCEPT
> When you acknowledge contributions, admit mistakes freely, and shine the light on others, everyone wins.

A Legendary Example of This Trait

John Wooden is widely regarded as the greatest college basketball coach in history—although he would never say that himself. His athletes won 665 games in 27 seasons, and 10 NCAA titles during his last 12 tries, 7 of them consecutively. "A player who makes a team great is more valuable than a great player. Losing yourself in the group, for the good of the group, that is teamwork." His simple philosophies have become legendary, his seven-point creed showing exactly who he is. Although he is regarded as one of the best of the very, very best there ever was in terms of team coaching, his mantras include helping others, giving thanks, and making friendship a fine art. For his ability to bring out the best in others without needing to take all of the credit, John Wooden has left a legacy of leadership with grace.

TO LEAVE A LEGACY:
1. Monitor Your Ego
2. Check In With Yourself
3. Champion Others

1. Monitor Your Ego

We all have egos. It is part of the human condition. But some egos are larger than others. Whether we like it or not, none of us is irreplaceable. Life does carry on without us. Don't let your ego get in the way of your ability to make the best choices. Keep your own sense of self-importance in perspective.

2. Check In With Yourself

In Achiever Trait 1: Ask Yourself Questions, we challenged you to use questions to stay connected to yourself and what you want to achieve. In this Legacy Trait, we build on that idea and ask you to ask yourself questions to stay connected to others and the larger goal. We can hold ourselves back from acting with humility for so many different reasons—we want to look great in other people's eyes, we try to hide mistakes, we need to have all of the credit. Having humility doesn't mean you aren't proud; it just means taking a more modest approach that comes from the security of knowing the role you played without needing all of the fanfare.

MARK: *Sebastian Coe is a highly distinguished athlete and politician. As a middle distance runner, Coe won four Olympic medals, including the gold in 1500 meters in 1980 and again in 1984. Following his retirement from athletics, he served as a Member of Parliament in Britain. He was the head of the London bid to host the 2012 Summer Olympics, and after the International Olympic Committee awarded the games to London, became the chairman of the London Organizing Committee for the Olympic Games (LOCOG).*

LEGACY

One year out from the start of the games, LOCOG hosted a seminar for the sport leaders of all of the 200-plus countries competing in London. It gave the heads of the various delegations a chance to see the venues and ask probing questions that related to preparations for their teams. At the very end of the weeklong meetings, Sebastian Coe took the stage. Coe was a track superstar. He could have had a huge ego. But he didn't. He spent most of his time singling out and thanking individual members of his team. He downplayed his own role, joking that he actually had very little to do. But, he also acknowledged the enormous challenges they face, appropriately so as the 2011 riots were playing out in this host city. The London Games have included the idea of legacy into every part of their delivery plan, but one of the most powerful legacies was the humility and commitment to the larger goal shown by the leader and his willingness to highlight the contribution of others throughout the organization.

3. Champion Others

There is a great ripple effect in being able to shine the light on others. When you move from a *me*-centered to a *we*-centered focus, you are able to stand back and marvel at being part of something great. You are connected not just to the outcome, but also to other people.

In Leader Trait 3: Create Synergy, we asked you to build great teams. In this Legacy Trait, we want you to lose yourself in the group, for the good of the group. It allows for mistakes to be made, for others to contribute, and for everyone to shine.

DEBBIE: For several years, as part of the team working for Own The Podium (OTP), I was able to use my experience in coaching athletes to Olympic and world championship gold medals to help other coaches. The whole philosophy of OTP is to focus funding on medal-potential sports and athletes, and sometimes in our intense focus on sport organizations, we overlook the people who actually connect the athletes to world-class performances day in and day out—the coaches.

Often when a coach is in the trenches with a talented athlete, there is no one out there to champion the great work they are doing, or to be an advocate for them to ensure they get what *they* need to meet their

LEGACY

challenges. We have learned a lot about how much an athlete must consider to win at the Olympics, and a coach has to do that much more. Coaches need support dealing with everything from getting the best physiotherapist for their athletes, to prioritizing program funding where money is spent, to coping with someone coming in and trying to tell them how to do their job. Because of my experience and the stature of the OTP program, I have been able to be a champion, to speak up for the needs of coaches and help protect the coaching environment so they can focus on being great at their job.

● TRAIT 4 REVIEW: Have Humility

TO LEAVE A LEGACY:
1. Monitor Your Ego
2. Check In With Yourself
3. Champion Others

KEY CONCEPT

When you acknowledge contributions, admit mistakes freely, and shine the light on others, everyone wins.

REALITY CHECK!

Sometimes we can overestimate our own importance, forgetting that with us or not, life carries on. The biggest limiting factor is that our egos get in the way, and we can't deny that we all have an ego. We don't want to make a mistake, or to step back and let others get credit, because we think this reflects badly on us. That is why when we actually do step back and let other people shine, or when we admit a mistake easily, when we really have humility, we make such a positive impression.

Bring This Trait to Life

To make a difference, consider the following:

- Are there times when a feeling of self-importance might be limiting you?
- Do you give credit when credit is due?
- Who do you support, advocate, and champion?

LEGACY

Show
Goodwill

TRAIT 5

TRAIT 5:
Show Goodwill

KEY CONCEPT
The way you respond, react, or simply are in situations
can have an enormous impact on those around you.

A Legendary Example of This Trait

*Jimmy Carter was the 39th president of the United States, and is recognized
today for his 25 years of writing, peacekeeping, and humanitarian efforts
since he left office. He is involved in many national and international
committees on public policy, conflict resolution, and human rights. He
is a best selling author and a Nobel Peace Prize winner. He and his
wife, Rosalynn, are well known for their work as volunteers for Habitat
for Humanity, a program that helps low-income working people build
and purchase their own homes. Seen hammering away, smiling at the
other volunteers, Jimmy Carter exudes the goodwill that has humanized
his legacy.*

TO LEAVE A LEGACY:
1. Give People the Benefit of the Doubt
2. Be Kind
3. Notice How You Touch Others

1. Give People the Benefit of the Doubt

The world is not a perfect place. As you encounter people, it is easy to criticize, to find faults, to draw attention to mistakes, and to put others down. It takes more of a conscious effort to give people the benefit of the doubt, to be positive and gracious unless you find out differently.

2. Be Kind

Something about the fast pace of our modern society has left the simple act of kindness behind. Acting curt, short-tempered, and rude have almost become acceptable ways of being. In Achiever Trait 5: Go the Distance, we asked you to dig deep to get through tough times and reach your own goals. In this Legacy Trait, we ask you to dig deeper to be kind to others to encourage them on their own journeys.

DEBBIE: I travel a lot for work, and sometimes it can be extremely gruelling. On a recent trip, I had the worst experience. I had flown across the country to a city I had never been to, and upon arriving, I had to rent a car so I could drive another couple of hours to get to my final destination. The instructions from the airport to the rental car places were very confusing, and as the evening was getting late, I found myself completely lost. Where I was supposed to go was across a major freeway but, to get there, I had to backtrack all the way to the airport terminal and then start all over again. On top of the time I had already lost, this was going to take another hour.

I was at my wit's end when I noticed a car rental shuttle bus arriving. It was for another company, and since I needed to go over to one of their competitors, when I first asked the driver if there was any way he could take me, I was met with a firm no. But, when the driver saw how desperate I was and there were no clients for him to worry about, he changed his

mind and very kindly offered me a ride. On the way over, I thanked him profusely. "You have made my day," I told him. "Well, you made mine back," he replied. "You just made my shift way less boring and I was able to help you at the same time."

3. Notice How You Touch Others

Goodwill can be as simple as smiling, saying thank you, or being polite and courteous in other ways. It is about building bridges instead of tearing them down, extending a hand instead of walking away. In Leader Trait 5: Communicate Effectively, we asked you to notice what came back to you in terms of communication. This Legacy Trait builds on that and asks you to pay attention to what comes back to you in terms of goodwill. See how it spreads.

MARK: *Although I was a great swimmer, I was never a big sports fan. I loved the Olympics, was glued to the television every four years when they were on, and that was it. In the months following my win in Barcelona, I was invited to numerous events, most of them with other high-profile athletes. The problem was that I didn't know who any of them were. At an Easter Seals fundraiser, I sat beside a young girl who was the poster child that year for the organization. Known as Little Tammy, her real name was Myroslava. Although she had physical challenges, she was the most outgoing sports fan I had ever met. She kept asking me to match the athlete she named with a sport and I inevitably always got it wrong. We laughed and joked all night long.*

About 10 years later, I was speaking at an event in Saskatchewan, and the organizers told me they had a surprise for me. Someone from my past wanted to see me. I looked across the room, and could see a young woman walking with a slight limp toward where I was standing. As she got closer, I recognized the girl from the banquet. She had grown into a beautiful young woman. She smiled the biggest smile when she arrived, and told me, "Mark, I never forgot you." I asked why. "Because you were one of the few people that year when I was Little Tammy who treated me like Myroslava." It made me reflect. What had I done? I was simply friendly, kind, and had some fun with another person. And that was enough to be remembered.

LEGACY

● TRAIT 5 REVIEW: Show Goodwill

TO LEAVE A LEGACY:
1. Give People the Benefit of the Doubt
2. Be Kind
3. Notice How You Touch Others

KEY CONCEPT

The way you respond, react, or simply are in situations can have an enormous impact on those around you.

REALITY CHECK!

We get so ingrained in our own lives that we just don't take the time to see how easy it is to give someone a smile, or go a bit out of our way to do something nice for another person. We get too caught up in our checklist of activities to show goodwill. But when you do, what comes back in terms of feeling good about yourself, you just can't put a price tag on.

Bring This Trait to Life

To make a difference, consider the following:

- Were you thoughtful and considerate today?
- Did you notice how your actions touched people around you?
- How does it make you feel when someone shows you goodwill?

Celebrate
Humanity

● TRAIT 6

TRAIT 6:
Celebrate
Humanity

KEY CONCEPT
It is important to remember that we share common
ground as human beings and, at the same time,
we are all different and unique.

A Legendary Example of This Trait

*Bono is best known as the lead singer and principal lyricist of the Irish
rock band, U2. But he is also recognized on the world stage as someone
who is dedicated to making a difference for people. Beginning in 1979 at
a benefit concert, his activism has led not only to songwriting motivated
by political, social, and religious themes; he has taken significant action.
Widely known for his work concerning Africa, he has been campaigning
since 1999 for Third World debt relief, meeting with political world leaders, and raising awareness for the injustices on the African continent. Well
beyond the Grammys, Bono has made an impact championing the rights
of other people, which has earned him an honorary knighthood, TIME
Person of the Year, and three nominations for the Nobel Peace Prize.*

TO LEAVE A LEGACY:
1. Acknowledge Diversity
2. Respect Differences
3. Connect With Others

1. Acknowledge Diversity

It is impossible to live in our hyper-connected world of communication today and NOT see that there is an abundance of diversity. We live on different continents; we come from different countries and traditions; we are various ages, genders, sexualities, and colors; and we belong to different socio-economic classes. Celebrating humanity begins by recognizing and acknowledging the vast diversity of our species.

2. Respect Differences

If everyone looked, thought, and behaved the same, we would get tired of being with each other. From the global macro level to the personal micro level, all of us are slightly different from each other. In Achiever Trait 2: Expand Your Perspective, we asked you to open yourself up to seeing things differently to create more possibility for yourself. In this Legacy Trait, we ask you to open yourself to see things differently so that you can respect differing points of view. Step outside of your own comfort zone and what your own culture has ingrained into you to see the validity of other perspectives.

DEBBIE: For many years, a good friend of mine wanted to stop renting and finally own a home. He lives in a city where real estate is sold at auction, and every time he had his heart set on a place, a higher offer would prevail and he would be on the losing end of the bid. One day he got an idea to look in a different part of the city, one that was more affordable for him but also less attractive to other buyers because it was a bit run-down. His idea worked and he finally had his home.

At first, many friends questioned his decision, seeing only the poverty and homelessness that seemed to plague his new neighborhood. After visiting him for a couple of years, I have been impressed at how the diversity of the area has actually served its inhabitants well. The young professionals who are upgrading their homes cohabitate peacefully with those who live in the shelters or boarding houses scattered throughout the area. Neighbors purposefully leave empty bottles on their front steps, knowing they will be taken by those who need them. A large group has even come together to petition the city to improve living conditions for some of their underprivileged neighbors who live in social housing. They have created a powerful local legacy of people looking out for each other.

3. Connect With Others

While each and every one of us is unique, collectively we share common ground. In Leader Trait 7: Embrace Contradictions, we asked you to accept the nature of paradox and see that opposite ideas can work together. In this Legacy Trait, we ask you to see that we are all different and, at the same time, we are all connected. A person is a person is a person is a person. We eat, we sleep, we love, we live. We cannot measure how well we are doing without measuring how well the whole world is doing. When diversity is truly respected and nurtured, then we have an opportunity to share who we are for the benefit of all.

MARK: *When I was part of the University of Calgary Swim Club, my teammates and I were invited to attend a Special Olympic competition to hand out medals. My experience in sport had been preoccupied with the idea of winning, so when I was at the pool and saw a gold medalist ask a silver medalist if they could swap once the ceremony was over because he already had "one of those gold ones," all I could do was laugh. Talk about a different perspective!*

The Special Olympics is an organization that provides a community via sport for people living with an intellectual disability. Over 40 years ago, a Canadian academic, Frank Hayden, brought the research to show that these kids who had historically been shut away at the back of the house would actually do well by exercising. Eunice Kennedy Shriver lent her celebrity to the idea, and a movement was born. For over 20 years, I have been involved in many different roles with the Special Olympics. Year after year, I learn something. Where an intellectual challenge is present, there is also often an outpouring of heart. It is the spirit in which these athletes compete that constantly connects me to my own humanity, and reminds me how much better I am to have been able to spend time with them.

● TRAIT 6 REVIEW: Celebrate Humanity

TO LEAVE A LEGACY:
1. Acknowledge Diversity
2. Respect Differences
3. Connect With Others

KEY CONCEPT

It is important to remember that we share common ground as human beings and, at the same time, we are all different and unique.

REALITY CHECK!

Human nature has two equal and opposite sides. One side is to celebrate humanity, the other is to attack difference. We believe that differences need to be recognized, supported, and celebrated. It is not about everybody trying to be the same. The tough part is that our own culture is ingrained in us, and it is hard to step outside of that and see the validity of other perspectives. The more we can do that, the richer and more multidimensional our celebration of humanity makes us.

Bring This Trait to Life

To make a difference, consider the following:

- What makes you and those around you unique?
- How do you champion and celebrate those qualities?
- Are you creating the space for others to share their cultures and experiences?

LEGACY

TRAIT 7:
Live Now

KEY CONCEPT

Accept where you are—whatever it looks like and however
it feels; this moment is exactly as it should be.

A Legendary Example of This Trait

*Richard Branson is an entrepreneur best known for the hip Virgin brand
all over the world. A man who has never waited for anything to happen,
he began his empire at 16 when he published his first magazine,* Student.
*By 21, he had already set up a mail-order business and a chain of record
stores. The Virgin brand was born on the spot, when all of the young
partners were "virgins" in business. Every moment of his life seems to
be spent doing something extraordinary beyond business—from chasing
and breaking world records in ballooning and amphibious vehicles, funding The Elders (a collective of former world leaders who use their skills
to catalyze peaceful resolutions), to investing an estimated $3 billion in
research for environmentally friendly fuels. Richard Branson's ability to
completely embrace life wherever he finds himself is where his legacy lies.*

TO LEAVE A LEGACY:
1. Embrace the Moment
2. Maximize Your Thinking
3. Make It Count

1. Embrace the Moment

This moment is as it is. Sometimes that might be a good thing, other times it might be a huge challenge. Remember, moments come and go. By embracing what is happening right now, you come to understand that there are things you can control, and things that you can't. You are not dwelling in the past or yearning for the future; you are simply in this moment, making the most out of wherever you find yourself.

MARK: *My family is huge on Christmas. We always have been—and everything, from decorations and food to the tree and presents, has always been a big and fun deal with my family. That also means that missing it, even to this day, is a pretty big deal.*

I remember one year, soon after my father had passed away, I wasn't going to be able to be home for the holidays because we were going to spend time with my partner's family. We were all really disappointed, but my mom in particular was hit hard. I ended up being in Calgary on December 11th, and a great idea hit me. Let's have Christmas tonight! I called Mom. It was 4 p.m. She loved the idea. She called my sister, and we were off to the races. We put up the tree; I bought gifts for under $20 for everyone, and Mom cooked a turkey loaf. We were giddy the whole time, hardly believing that when we woke up that morning, none of us could have imagined this. Here we were—we made Christmas happen two weeks early.

2. Maximize Your Thinking

It can be easy to put life on hold, or even feel like a victim. We think when things are better—when we have more money, more time, more space, more *something*—then our life will magically be better. In Achiever Trait 7: Utilize Power of Thought, we looked at the influence that our thinking has on our actions and results. This Legacy Trait builds on that to ask, "What are you specifically thinking in this moment?" Living now means understanding that you have the power to make the most out of the things you can control in your life.

DEBBIE: The Vancouver 2010 Opening Ceremony provided a global platform to recognize Rick Hansen, and remind us of the huge legacy he has created by making the most out of his circumstance. At 15, Rick was an all-star athlete in Port Alberni, British Columbia, when an auto accident led to a spinal cord injury that left him paralyzed from the waist down. Following rehabilitation, Rick decided to continue on the path his life was heading, only this time in a wheelchair.

Rick played wheelchair volleyball and basketball, and he became a world-class marathoner. He became the first student with a physical disability to graduate in physical education from the University of British Columbia. In 1985, Rick set out on his Man in Motion World Tour (MIM-WT), a 26-month trek that saw him log in 40,000 kilometers through 34 countries and raise $26 million for spinal cord research. In 2011, Rick launched the 25th Anniversary Man in Motion Tour, this time inviting 7,000 everyday heroes to take part in a cross-Canada relay with him. An ongoing advocate for people with spinal cord injuries, Rick Hansen is a living example of taking the moment and making the most of it.

3. Make It Count

In Leader Trait 2: Have Purpose, we looked at the importance of working toward a goal that has a sense of awe. This Legacy Trait builds on that by ensuring you don't wait for the future to come; you make it happen by living now with a sense of purpose in all that you do. This is it. Find out what makes you feel inspired, excited and alive, and then act on it—make it count *now*.

LEGACY

● TRAIT 7 REVIEW: Live Now

TO LEAVE A LEGACY:
1. Embrace the Moment
2. Maximize Your Thinking
3. Make It Count

KEY CONCEPT

Accept where you are—whatever it looks like and however it feels; this moment is exactly as it should be.

REALITY CHECK!

It is so easy to get caught up in dreaming of a future that doesn't yet exist, or worrying about what has happened in the past, that we completely forget about the time we have in front of us right here and now. We know that this is a little bit of a contradiction because most of this book has been about planning for the future and defining your desired outcome. The irony is that the way to get there is to be here and live now. When you can do that, you are able to accept this moment, knowing it is as it should be, and at the same time, you can live now to make it become whatever you would like it to be.

Bring This Trait to Life

To make a difference, consider the following:

- Right now, in this moment, where is your thinking?
- Are you accepting this current moment as it is?
- Are you making the most of where you are?

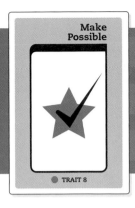

TRAIT 8:
Make Possible

KEY CONCEPT
When we embody the "why not?" attitude for ourselves
and for others, we find a way forward, no matter what.

A Legendary Example of This Trait

Bill Gates is an entrepreneur and philanthropist. Best known as the chairman of Microsoft, and one of the titans of the personal computer revolution, he made it possible for the technology that has advanced communication beyond our wildest imaginations. He has become a champion of numerous important causes. With his wife, Melinda, he has established the Bill and Melinda Gates Foundation, following in the tradition of the Rockefellers, Carnegies, and others. Supported by Warren Buffet, Gates is donating large amounts of money to various charitable organizations and scientific research programs. Bill Gates is helping to make opportunities possible for underrepresented minorities, and to prevent AIDS and other prevalent diseases in Third World countries.

TO LEAVE A LEGACY:
1. Say Yes to Possibility
2. Wake Up to Potential
3. Find Ways Forward

1. Say Yes to Possibility

Each of us will find ourselves at one time or another in a situation that seems impossible to overcome. The easy way out is to make excuses or run away and jump ship. It might *seem* easier to be negative and cynical—to give up—but what kind of a message does that send? When you come at every situation with an open mind, knowing that there is always a solution to be found, you say yes to possibility.

DEBBIE: We don't often come together in Canada as a nation in grief, but the death of Jack Layton united Canadians coast to coast. Coming from a family with a long history of political activism and service, Jack rode to prominence in the 1980s as a member of Toronto's city council. An author, professor, and outspoken advocate, Jack was the voice for the people. He got individuals and communities involved, not with politics but with his personality. A guitar-playing, storytelling, deeply engaged person, Jack captured the hearts and trust of Canadians.

In 2011, with Jack at the lead, the New Democratic Party became the Official Opposition in the House of Commons of Canada. It was a triumph for a man who never stopped believing in his cause, and knew that with an open mind and spirit, you can take on anything. When his death from cancer on August 22nd was publicly announced, the outpouring of appreciation and gratitude came immediately from supporters and opponents alike. Jack's optimism and hope had struck a nerve. Even in his last message to Canadians, we saw the eternal positive attitude that embodied this political leader. In his own words, "My friends, love is better than anger. Hope is better than fear. Optimism is better than despair. So let us be strong, hopeful, and optimistic. And together we'll change the world."

2. Wake Up to Potential

The biggest thing holding you back might be yourself. It can be easy to get complacent and limit yourself in terms of what is possible. In Leader Trait 8: Continually Evolve, we asked you to raise the bar to continue growing and improving. This Legacy Trait builds on that idea by asking you to wake up to your own potential. Don't underestimate the difference you can make with your life, for yourself and others. There are no limits, only the ones you perceive.

3. Find Ways Forward

Sometimes in life, the circumstances you need to succeed are not actually there when you need them. In Achiever Trait 6: Be Innovative, we asked you to tap into your own unique history to find new ways forward. We build on that idea in this Legacy Trait by asking you to not only tap into your own experience, but to be inspired by the unique experiences of those around you and those who have come before. Think of all the people who made things possible for you, and the people who you have made things possible for. What circumstances were created to find a way forward? If the environment isn't there for success to happen, create it.

MARK: *I want to take you back to where this book started. It was over 20 years ago, when Debbie and I formed our friendship and partnered together in what would eventually become Great Traits Inc. She was the retired synchronized swimming coach and I was the speed swimmer, coming together to try to win the Olympics.*

I remember when it looked like we might work together, I told Debbie flat out that there were three things we needed to overcome: 1) I have no money (making $650 per month); 2) I have no time (How do we fit this extra work in—I am already more than full time); 3) I have no support (What will my coach and team do?). Debbie's answer, beyond asking me to communicate openly with my coach and team, was simple. "We will find a way. We will make it work." And we always have.

● TRAIT 8 REVIEW: Make Possible

TO LEAVE A LEGACY:
1. Say Yes to Possibility
2. Wake Up to Potential
3. Find Ways Forward

KEY CONCEPT

When we embody the "why not?" attitude for ourselves and for others, we find a way forward, no matter what.

REALITY CHECK!

It is easy to focus on all of the things that we can't do, what might go wrong, what will work against us. And often, with all of these ideas in our head, we stop ourselves before we even start. Making possible means staying open to the thousands and thousands of little things that we can do. It means remembering that embodying the "why not?" attitude will ensure that some solution always presents itself, and makes possibilities appear for yourself and others.

Bring This Trait to Life

To make a difference, consider the following:

- Are you able to find a way through, in spite of the challenges or odds against you?
- If the circumstances aren't there to do what needs to be done, are you creating ones that will?
- Are you championing the way of life that you want to see happen for yourself and others?

KEY CONCEPT SYNOPSIS
THE LEGACY TRAITS
Championing a Meaningful Way of Life

 Your values act as a compass that guides your decision making and shows people who you are.

 The way you respond, react, or simply are in situations can have an enormous impact on those around you.

 Having the courage to challenge popular ideas often leads to break-throughs for yourself and others.

 It is important to remember that we share common ground as human beings and, at the same time, we are all different and unique.

 Recognize the impact you have with your life by sharing your wisdom, experience, and knowledge with others.

 Accept where you are—whatever it looks like and however it feels; this moment is as it should be.

 When you acknowl-edge contributions, admit mistakes freely, and shine the light on others, everyone wins.

 When we embody the "why not?" attitude for ourselves and others, we find a way forward, no matter what.

LEGACY TRAITS—SELF-ASSESSMENT

Before moving on in this book, take the time to think about how you live each of the Legacy Traits. See what traits need more work than others and invest some time in them. This isn't about a rating scale. It is about awareness, and understanding how you bring each of the traits to life.

Legacy Trait

1. Embody Values

 How do I bring this trait to life?

2. Challenge Convention

 How do I bring this trait to life?

3. Influence Wisely

 How do I bring this trait to life?

4. Have Humility

 How do I bring this trait to life?

Legacy Trait

5. Show Goodwill

How do I bring this trait to life?

6. Celebrate Humanity

How do I bring this trait to life?

7. Live Now

How do I bring this trait to life?

8. Make Possible

How do I bring this trait to life?

LEGACY

YOUR CHAMPION'S JOURNEY CONTINUES!

This concludes the *Great Traits of Champions*, and we hope you have enjoyed it. But the *Champion's Journey* never ends. We hope you take the traits and apply them to everything you do.

You have experienced what it means to be a champion from three distinct perspectives.

In the first section, the Achiever Traits connected you to the idea of being great at whatever it is you do, and ensured the fundamental ideas are in place to build the skills necessary for you to succeed. The Leader Traits laid the foundation for you to create the environment for others—individuals, teams, and organizations—to succeed. Finally, the Legacy Traits challenged you to consciously maximize your impact for the benefit of all. Achieving and leading are important, but it is equally vital to consider what kind of difference you are making along the way.

Throughout this book, we outlined each trait individually in a methodical and linear fashion. The reality is that life is not about boxes and silos: it is much more fluid than that! As you probably see by now, the Great Traits work like this, too.

Every individual trait has its own unique focus, and at the same time can work in conjunction with the other 23 traits. Essentially, they are all related to each other. That is where we think the magic really lies. The simple ideas become deceptively powerful when they work together. And now that you know all of the Great Traits, the fun can really begin.

The more you use the Great Traits, the more dynamic they become. You will find that the right traits start to come to mind in any given situation. When you are feeling disconnected, you might go to Achiever Trait 1: Ask Yourself Questions, or Leader Trait 2: Have Purpose. When you are tired and feel like giving up, you might go to Achiever Trait 5: Go the Distance, or Leadership Trait 5: Show Conviction. We could go on and on, but you get the idea. Ironically, it is the simplicity of the traits that allows them to adapt to the complexities of life. They really work!

As we said at the beginning of this journey, we do not think we know it all. We will always keep learning and having new experiences. What we know to this point, we have shared with you here.

Our objective is to provide what we believe are the building blocks to succeed in the areas we have experienced extensively: achievement, leadership, and legacy. What made these ideas powerful was bringing them to life. And that is the final thing we ask of you.

Apply what we have learned from our experience into something meaningful for you.

This is where your *Champion's Journey* really starts...

KEY CONCEPT SYNOPSIS
THE ACHIEVER TRAITS
Fundamentals for Being a Champion

 By becoming a master of the question, you stay connected to yourself and to what you want to achieve.

 On the way to achieving your desired win, you must be willing to persist through tough times and periods of hard work.

 By looking at circumstances differently, you access new realms of possibility for yourself.

 By challenging yourself to tap into new ideas, you find unique solutions to move forward.

 By laying the foundation for focused action, you create a clear path to take you to your desired win.

 By mastering your thoughts, you have a much greater chance of accessing your full potential.

 By aligning your day-to-day actions with your objectives, you ensure that what you are doing will keep you on track.

 Since we rarely achieve anything alone, by sharing your passion and excitement you invite others to be a part of the journey.

KEY CONCEPT SYNOPSIS
THE LEADER TRAITS
Creating Champion Organizations and Teams

 The greater your awareness, the greater your capacity to act effectively as a leader.

 By creating an environment where direction is clear and opinions are freely shared, people are engaged and feel part of the process.

 By capturing people's imagination with clear objectives and roles, you inspire everyone to do their part in making it happen.

 By using the power of your example, you inspire excellence in others.

 By bringing together the right people, an inexplicable energy is created that produces winning results much greater than any one individual's contribution.

 By being open to various possibilities in any given situation, you can find what works even if that appears to contradict what you have done before.

 By believing completely in what you are doing, it enables you and those you lead to achieve outstanding results.

 By creating a dynamic environment where the bar is constantly being raised, excellence is fostered and winning results happen.

KEY CONCEPT SYNOPSIS
THE LEGACY TRAITS
Championing a Meaningful Way of Life

 Your values act as a compass that guides your decision making and shows people who you are.

 Having the courage to challenge popular ideas often leads to breakthroughs for yourself and others.

 Recognize the impact you have with your life by sharing your wisdom, experience, and knowledge with others.

 When you acknowledge contributions, admit mistakes freely, and shine the light on others, everyone wins.

 The way you respond, react, or simply are in situations can have an enormous impact on those around you.

 It is important to remember that we share common ground as human beings and, at the same time, we are all different and unique.

 Accept where you are—whatever it looks like and however it feels; this moment is as it should be.

 When we embody the "why not?" attitude for ourselves and others, we find a way forward, no matter what.

NOTES

NOTES

NOTES

NOTES

NOTES

NOTES

NOTES

NOTES

NOTES